Doing Research in Further Education and Training

Doing Research in Further Education and Training

Susan Wallace

Los Angeles | London | New Delhi
Singapore | Washington DC

Learning Matters An imprint of SAGE
Publications Ltd 1 Oliver's Yard 55 City
Road London EC1Y 1SP

SAGE Publications Inc. 2455 Teller Road
Thousand Oaks, California 91320

SAGE Publications India Pvt Ltd B 1/I 1
Mohan Cooperative Industrial Area Mathura
Road New Delhi 110 044

SAGE Publications Asia-Pacific Pte Ltd
3 Church Street
#102-04 Samsung Hub
Singapore 049483

Editor: Amy Thornton
Development editor: Clare Weaver
Production controller: Chris Marke
Project management: Deer Park
Productions, Tavistock
Marketing manager: Catherine Slinn
Cover design: Topics
Typeset by: PDQ Typesetting Ltd,
Staffordshire
Printed in Great Britain by MPG Printgroup,
UK

Library of Congress Control Number:
2013934047

British Library Cataloguing in Publication
data
A catalogue record for this book is available
from the British Library

ISBN 978 1 44625 918 4
ISBN 978 1 44625 919 1 (pbk)

MIX
Paper from
responsible sources
FSC® C018575
www.fsc.org
FSC

Contents

About the author

Susan Wallace is Professor of Continuing Education at Nottingham Trent University where she is responsible for mentoring newly appointed staff in the School of Education. Having previously worked for ten years in the FE sector and in a local authority advisory role for post-16 education, she has published extensively on the professional development of teachers and trainers.

1
Why do it? How doing research can support teaching and learning

The objectives of this chapter

This chapter looks at ways in which research – from very small scale to more ambitious projects – can inform our ideas for teaching and learning, and how we can use the findings to improve the quality of the learning experience. It draws on examples from the context of Further Education and Training to illustrate these uses of research, and it also introduces and explains some key research terminology, including: *source*; *data*; *reliability*; *trustworthiness*; *validity*; *triangulation*; *desktop research*; *secondary sources*; *empirical research*; *primary sources*; *qualitative*; *quantitative*; and *mixed methods*.

Introduction

Why might we, as teachers, want to carry out research in Further Education (FE) and vocational training? One possible reason, of course, is that some research activity may be required in order to complete an initial teacher training, continuing professional development (CPD) or Masters assignment. But then we still have to ask ourselves why such a requirement would be necessary. And there are two very clear answers to this question. One is that research is an extension of the process of reflection on practice and is therefore an activity which is central to our role as professionals. The other is that research is an essential tool for raising and maintaining the quality of learning and teaching. It can be used as a means of looking for solutions to difficulties or dilemmas we might face in the classroom, such as how to raise levels of learner engagement or deal effectively with lack of punctuality. It allows us to investigate the impact of policy innovations on practices in our own institution. And it also provides a means of keeping up to date with ideas and developments in our own subject area. In this chapter and the ones that follow we're going to look at all these ways in which research can be used to support our professional skills, knowledge and understanding. To do that, we'll be looking at some 'real life' cases and exploring the purposes, practicalities and applications of practitioner research in FE and vocational training.

TASK TASK TASK TASK TASK TASK TASK TASK

Read the account of Sara's dilemma below and consider the following questions:

1. Can we call what Sara does here 'research'? If so, why? If you think not, what are your reasons?

2. Is Sara using an appropriate *source* here for the information she is seeking? The source she chooses is the group of latecomers themselves. Are there any other sources of information she could have used, or any alternative ways of obtaining answers from the latecomers?

3. How *trustworthy* or *reliable* is the information which Sara gathers in this way? What means could she use to double check whether what the latecomers are telling her is actually the case?

4. Assuming that the information she now has is accurate, how can Sara use it: a) to improve the quality of teaching and learning in this class; and b) to support her own professional development?

You may find it useful to make a note of your answers before going on to read the Discussion which follows.

Sara teaches a level 2 group of 16–17-year-olds. There are 19 students on the register, ten male and nine female. The class is scheduled to run from 10 a.m. until 11.30 a.m. each Wednesday. However, Sara finds she is losing almost 30 minutes from each class because of some students turning up late, in ones and twos, throughout the first half hour. At first she chose to recap and repeat lesson content for each latecomer, on the basis that they would be unable to benefit from the rest of the lesson unless they had a clear idea of what had gone before. But now she finds she is running out of time to cover the required curriculum content, and so she decides that something must be done. But what will be the most effective way to deal with this problem? She has left herself no time for a trial and error approach, and so she comes to the conclusion that the first step to a fast and effective solution must be to discover the learners' reasons for arriving late. The following Wednesday she makes a note of the names of the latecomers. There are six of them, all girls, and they are the usual suspects. She asks them to stay for a moment after the class and she asks them, as a group, to explain to her why they are habitually late. It's clear at first that they assume this is a 'telling off', and they don't have much constructive to say. But Sara perseveres. She tries changing her question and asks them instead, *'What would make you arrive in time for the start of the lesson?'* Their answers take her by surprise. They tell her that they would turn up on time if they thought she would notice, but that she only takes notice of the boys, so what's the point? Shocked, she asks them to explain. *'The boys get all your attention,'* one girl tells her, *'and you always spend the first bit of the lesson making sure they've remembered stuff from last time. So it's boring.'*

Whatever response Sara was expecting, it certainly wasn't this. She'll need to go away and think about this carefully.

Discussion
Let's look at the questions now and answer each of them as fully as we can.

1. *Can we call what Sara does here 'research'? If so, why? If you think not, what are your reasons?*

Although what Sara does here is spontaneous and informal, we can still call it research. The clue is in that phrase: *'to discover why'*. Sara sets out to discover why some learners are habitually late for that class. She decides what she considers to be the best source for this information – the latecomers themselves. She frames a research question: *'Why are you habitually late?'* And then, finding this unproductive, she re-frames it: *'What would make you arrive in time for the start of the lesson?'* And she obtains her information, which – in research terminology – we may call her data. So what we see here is recognisably a research model. Of course, it is a very rough and ready one. If Sara were to write this up as a formal research project she would find it open to criticism on several points, as we shall see as we go through the rest of the questions. Nevertheless, she shows us here at a basic

level how an FE teacher can take on the role of researcher as an integral part of her professional practice.

2. *Is Sara using an appropriate* **source** *here for the information she is seeking? The
source she chooses is the group of latecomers themselves. Are there any other
sources of information she could have used, or any alternative ways of obtaining
answers from the latecomers?*

Let's be clear, first of all, about what information Sara is seeking. She wants to know *why*
some learners habitually turn up late for her class. It's clear, then, that the learners themselves
are an appropriate place to start looking for answers. The extent to which Sara can *trust* their
answers will be discussed in the next question; but for her to attempt to solve this puzzle
without asking them at all would not really make much sense. In research terms, therefore,
we can describe the data she gets from them as *valid*. That is, it is from an appropriate and
relevant source in the context of her research question. If she were to ask, let's say, her
newsagent on her way home why *he* thought this group of students was always late, his
response might be interesting, but it wouldn't constitute valid data because he wouldn't be in
a position to know anything about their circumstances or motivation.

She could, however, have considered other sources in addition to asking the learners
themselves. For example, she could have asked other teachers whether those particular
students were usually late for their sessions too. Or she could have asked her section head –
or the learners' personal tutor, if they have one – whether there are any circumstances in the
learners' lives which could be causing them to arrive late. Making use of these additional
sources of information would also allow her to compare what she discovered there with
what the learners themselves are telling her. This cross checking between one data source
and another is known as *triangulation*, and we'll be discussing its uses further in the next
question. Before we do, let's just consider some of the alternative methods Sara could have
used to obtain answers from the unpunctual learners. She could, for example, have taken a
more formal approach and designed a questionnaire to be completed by every learner in the
class who arrived after the start of the lesson. Or, if she had the time to spare, she could
interview each of the latecomers individually. Or she could have posed her question by
convening the latecomers more formally as a *focus group*. If she had been carrying out this
research as part of an initial teaching qualification, CPD or MA assignment, she would
probably have used one of these more structured methods of collecting her data, and
would be expected to give clear reasons justifying her choice (see Close Focus below).

3. *How* **trustworthy** *or* **reliable** *is the information which Sara gathers in this way? What
means could she use to double check whether what the latecomers are telling her is
actually the case?*

Sara will need to consider to what extent she can trust the data she has collected. Is the
learners' account of the situation 'true'? Would an objective observer see it in the same way?
In other words, is Sara really giving most of her attention to the boys in the class and so
making the girls feel left out; or are these girls exaggerating in order to give themselves an
excuse for being late? How *reliable* is their response as data? If someone else – not their
teacher – asked them why they were always late, would they give the same answer? And,
even if they really do believe that Sara is paying insufficient attention to the girls in the class,
might this simply be their perception – a very subjective view – which an objective observation would show to be untrue? These questions about the reliability and trustworthiness of
data are important ones that must be addressed in any research. It would be wise, therefore,

for Sara to double-check her findings. She might, for example, arrange to have her next couple of sessions with this group recorded to camera; or she might ask a colleague, mentor or tutor to sit in and observe her. She would then be able to compare those results with what these learners have told her, and see whether the two are consistent. This triangulation of methods would be a way of adding weight to the conclusions she is drawing from her research, and would be particularly useful if she were writing this up as a formal research project.

4. *Assuming that the information she now has is accurate, how can Sara use it: a) to improve the quality of teaching and learning in this class; and b) to support her own professional development?*

So let's imagine that Sara has asked her mentor to observe her next session with this group and to look out particularly for how Sara divides her attention between male and female learners; and let's assume that her mentor has confirmed what the unpunctual students said. Now that she is aware of her own tendency to speak more to the boys, Sara can consider ways to address this. It's likely that she will begin at once to monitor patterns of teacher– learner interactions in all her classes, and will look carefully at her lesson planning to devise teaching strategies and learning activities that engage all learners equally. She will probably ask the learners more regularly now for evaluative feedback, particularly on the issue of inclusion; and she will monitor punctuality in order to see whether all these measures are having the required effect. The research and its aftermath, in alerting her to the importance of inclusive practice, will have been valuable to her professional development. She may decide to make this issue a focus of her reflective journal, which will help her to maintain vigilance about inclusion in all the classes she teaches. And she may decide to do more research, this time in the form of some reading, perhaps, to discover what other teachers and researchers have to say about inclusion in relation to gender. We would call this last activity *desktop research* using *secondary sources*; while getting out there and asking questions as Sara did to start with is *empirical research* using *primary sources*.

CLOSE FOCUS ~~CLOSE FOCUS~~ CLOSE FOCUS ~~CLOSE FOCUS~~ CLOSE FOCUS

Let's look more closely here at what was said, in response to question 2, about the possible use of questionnaires or interviews. Sara might have decided to use either or both of these methods to collect her data, and it was mentioned that a more formal approach such as this would have been an advantage if she had been conducting the research as part of a project or assignment. Why do you think that would be so? Take some time to consider your answers to the following questions:

- What might be the advantages of giving individuals a written questionnaire to complete anonymously rather than informal oral questioning of a small group?
- What might be the advantages of conducting individual interviews rather than informally questioning a group?
- Which of these three methods – informal questioning, questionnaire, interview – do you think would be likely to yield the most *reliable* data, and why?
- What, in your view, might be the main disadvantage of each of these methods, and why?
- You may find it useful to keep a careful note of your answers. We shall be returning to these questions in Chapters 6 and 7, where we look at these methods in more detail.

Terminology

When we discuss things to do with research, even informally, it's useful to have a customised vocabulary that allows us to think and to talk about the subject accurately and clearly. Like other aspects of our professional role – assessment, teaching, lesson planning – research has its own specialised terms. So let's look again at the research terminology we've encountered so far and set out some working definitions:

- *Data:* The information that you collect during your research. It's worth noting here that *data* is the plural noun, like *children* or *fungi*. (The singular form, rarely used, is *datum*.) You'll therefore see it in sentences like this: 'The *data were* collected by questionnaire'. However, not everyone remembers this all the time, and so it can be a little confusing!
- *Reliability*: Data are considered reliable if they remain consistent whoever is collecting the data and at whatever time.
- *Trustworthiness:* Data have varying degrees of trustworthiness depending upon their source and the form they take. For example, the reason a learner gives to you, her teacher, face to face, for not completing her assignment may be different from the reason she would feel free to give if answering the same question anonymously in a questionnaire. The trustworthiness of data is about accuracy, however, and not always necessarily about honesty. Sara seems to assume that the answers (data) she gets from her unpunctual learners can be trusted. Perhaps you would be more cautious?
- *Validity:* Data are considered valid if they are from a source appropriate and relevant to the research question. For example, if you wanted to find out why learners had chosen to take the FE route rather than going into a school sixth form, you would be more likely to obtain valid data if you asked the learners themselves rather than asking their teachers to take a guess about the reasons for their learners' choice.
- *Triangulation:* A way of cross checking the reliability and trustworthiness of data, either by using more than one method of collecting it, or by asking the same question again but in a slightly different way. For example, a questionnaire might ask: 'Why did you choose to come to a College of Further Education?' and then, several questions later, 'Why did you choose not to stay on at school to continue your studies?' The responses can then be checked for consistency.
- *Empirical research:* Research which involves the collection and analysis of original data.
- *Desktop research:* Research which focuses on documentary analysis. Literally, it can be done without leaving your desk.
- *Source:* Where you get your data from.
- *Primary source:* A source of original data; that is, data which you have obtained directly and first hand rather than it having been selected and presented by someone else. For example, raw retention and attainment statistics are a primary source of data.
- *Secondary source:* A source of data which is second or third hand. For example, the Vice Principal's report which summarises those retention and attainment statistics is a secondary source because she's already analysed them and selected examples for presentation.

Qualitative research and quantitative research

When Sara did her quick little bit of research, the answers or data she collected were in the form of students' own explanations for their behaviour. We call data like this *'qualitative* data'. Such data do not provide us with 'facts' that are weighable or measurable, but focus instead on accounts of human experience, which is far less predictable, far less easily verifiable, and much more complex. Research which uses qualitative data is known as *qualitative research.*

If, on the other hand, Sara had taken a different approach and had decided to keep a record of which students were late and by how many minutes, she would have been collecting *quantitative* data. *Quantitative* research methods, as the term suggests, employ counting and measurement. They produce the sort of data that can be represented by graphs, tables and pie charts; the sort of data that are quantifiable – that is to say, can be expressed in terms of numbers.

Because learning, teaching and training focus largely on complex human behaviours, inter-actions, responses and values, educational research is often qualitative in its approach. If you wanted to explore the reason some learners give for disengaging from their learning, for example, a qualitative approach would be the most appropriate and would serve your purposes very well. If, on the other hand, you wanted to discover how many of those disengaged learners had achieved their English and Maths at grade C or above, you would need to do some counting and correlation – a piece of *quantitative* research.

TASK TASK **TASK** TASK **TASK** TASK **TASK** TASK **TASK** TASK

We're going to look now at how Kev, a student teacher, combines both these approaches when he carries out an investigative project as part of his teaching qualification coursework. While you're reading about what Kev gets up to, you should consider the following questions and make some notes so that you can compare your own answers to the discussion that follows:

- **What assumptions is Kev making in the way he phrases his first question?**
- **Are there alternative ways Kev could have collected his data?**
- **Are there other questions Kev could usefully have asked?**
- **Why do you think Kev makes the questionnaire anonymous?**
- **What other information would it be useful for us to know about Kev's sample group?**
- **What do you understand Kev's tutor to mean by 'mixed methods'?**

Kev is a student teacher doing a six-week period of teaching experience in a large College of Further Education. As part of his qualification he has an assignment to write which involves a small research project, and he has been thinking about what topic to choose. He has noticed that very few of the 16–18-year-old learners he has taught and observed make any effort to take notes during class, and he wonders whether this is because they don't choose to do it or because they have never acquired note-taking skills. Kev's been doing some reading around this which has persuaded him that students remember what they have been taught better if they have made a note of it themselves rather than being given a handout which they may or may not read. He would like, therefore, to encourage his own classes to take notes, but he knows he must first discover the extent of their note-taking skills. This seems like a perfect focus for his assignment, and so he decides to design a small research project around this topic. This is what he says about it:

'I realised this was something I needed to know more about. I saw it, I guess, as an area for professional development. There were two lots of information I wanted to collect. One was: *How many of the students had been taught anything about effective note-taking?* The other was: *What strategies did students use to help them to remember what they had been taught?* This second one seemed an important question to ask because, if they couldn't make notes, and they hadn't come up with an alternative way to help them retain knowledge, skills, etc., I would have evidence to support my argument that they should be taught note-taking as a matter of priority. This meant I was looking for two quite different sorts of data. The first sort was straightforwardly about numbers and would be easy to add up and summarise; but the second sort might produce a different answer from every student which would be more complex to analyse and draw conclusions from. My tutor said this was 'mixed methods' approach.

I collected the first, the quantitative data, by asking for a show of hands in the four classes I teach. I just asked, 'How many of you have been taught how to take notes, here at college or at school?' And then I counted up. It didn't take long! Two in one class, one in the other – so it was pretty much as I suspected. Then, to collect answers to my other question, I gave all the students in those two classes a very short questionnaire which they filled in anonymously. It just had two questions:

i)   What do you do to help yourself to remember what we have talked about and what you have learnt in this lesson?
ii) How well does it work for you, and why?

This qualitative data took much longer to go through and analyse, even though they had very little to say. Three of the responses said 'note-taking', which tallied with the data from the hand count – so that was good. But on the whole it looked as though the majority didn't do anything very productive or useful – so that sort of proved my point. And so now, as well as producing an interesting assignment, I've got the evidence to justify including a short input on note-taking skills in all my lesson plans!'

Discussion

- *What assumptions is Kev making in the way he phrases his first question?* To collect his quantitative data – numbers – Kev asks the students about whether they have *been taught* to make notes. He's making two assumptions here: that if they have been taught how to do it they will have retained that skill and be able to put it into practice; and that if they have not been taught how to take notes they won't be able to do it. Of course, neither of these is necessarily the case. So, because he's not quite thought this through properly, it could be that his data doesn't mean quite what he thinks it means.
- *Are there alternative ways Kev could have collected his data?* If, instead of asking for a show of hands, Kev had asked the learners to make notes of the main points while he was teaching a short part of his next session, and then he had collected their notes in, he would have had a more accurate idea of how many *possessed* note-taking skills, rather than how many had *been taught* note-taking skills (which we know is not the same thing!). This would have been more relevant to his purpose in carrying out the project.
- *Why do you think Kev makes the questionnaire anonymous?* Kev is probably assuming here that if individual learners know they cannot be identified they will be more likely to answer honestly, and therefore the data will be more reliable and trustworthy.
- *What other information would it be useful for us to know about Kev's sample group?* We know that there are two groups or classes, and we know that the learners are aged 16–18. But we don't know how many learners this sample contains in total, and so although we know that three have been taught note-taking, we don't have any indication of what this means as a proportion of the whole. If it were only three out of 100, for example, this would make Kev's argument carry more weight than if it was three out of 40.
- *What do you understand Kev's tutor to mean by 'mixed methods'?* We use this term to describe a research approach that combines the collection of quantitative and qualitative data. A mixed

methods approach is another way of building in triangulation, because you can compare the results obtained by one method with results obtained by another. If they're the same, you can feel reassured that your data are relatively reliable. You can see how useful Kev considers this to be when the two methods he uses each seems to show up the same number of learners who have learnt note-taking skills (although, as we've seen in the first discussion point above, he might be making too many assumptions here).

CLOSE FOCUS CLOSE FOCUS **CLOSE FOCUS** CLOSE FOCUS **CLOSE FOCUS**

Read Kev's account again together with the discussion which follows it and decide to what extent you would say that the data Kev collects overall are: a) reliable; and b) valid. What reasons would you give for your answers?

Being a subject specialist

We've looked now at two examples of research being used by teachers to understand, support and inform classroom practice in FE and training. But there is another way in which research skills are useful to us as practitioners in our profession. Each of us, as well as being a teacher, has a vocational or subject expertise which enables us to do the job that we do. Whether this is in electronics, health care, basic skills or business studies, it is part of our professional responsibility to keep ourselves up to date with the latest developments and ideas in our own subject area. This, too, is a form of research, whether we do it by *desktop*, reading through the latest trade journals or websites; or by *observation*, visiting people and organisations where such work is carried out; or by *interview*, talking to people in the trade. We may not formalise this research by 'writing it up', and we may not even *call* it 'research', but nevertheless it will inform our teaching by extending and challenging our subject knowledge.

A SUMMARY OF **KEY POINTS**

In this chapter we have looked at how research in FE and training can help us when:
> **looking for solutions to difficulties or dilemmas we might face in the classroom;**
> **finding ways to improve the quality of the learning experience;**
> **looking for ways to inform ideas for teaching and learning;**
> **identifying our own continuing professional development needs;**
> **keeping up to date with ideas and developments in our own subject area.**

We have also identified some useful words to use when talking about research. These include: *source; data; reliability; trustworthiness; validity; triangulation; desktop research; secondary sources; empirical research; primary sources; qualitative; quantitative; mixed methods.*

Branching options

You may like to choose one of the following activities which are designed to help you apply what you've learnt from this chapter to your own practice. The first encourages you, as a professional, to develop your skills of reflection; the second asks you to take an evaluative approach consistent with an initial teaching qualification in the sector; and the third is designed to support skills of critical analysis appropriate to post-qualification CPD or Masters level study.

Reflection

Using a search engine such as Google Scholar or the contents of TES Online, look and see what aspects of teaching and learning in FE have been most popular recently as research topics. For example, it might be *learner motivation*, or it might be *inclusion,* or perhaps it is *progression;* or it may be something else entirely. Whatever the topic, think about how this might relate to your own teaching. Is it something you, too, would identify as important to your own professional practice, and, if so, in what ways and why?

Evaluation

Think of an aspect of your recent classroom experience that you would like to explore. How would you phrase this as a research question? Who would you need to answer it? Write your question down and look at it carefully. Is it the right question to get you the sort of data you need? Is it clear and unambiguous? How would the answer to this question help to improve the quality of teaching and learning in your classes?

Critical analysis

Look again at Kev's account of his research. How trustworthy do you think his findings are? Are they, in your view, more trustworthy than Sara's data? What are the reasons for your answer? If Kev wanted to make a case for introducing note-taking skills to all classes across the college, what additional data might he need to make his argument convincing, and why?

FURTHER READING FURTHER READING **FURTHER READING** FURTHER READING

The following three books all give very clear accounts of the ideas and terminology we've encountered in this chapter, and are all very readable. Opie and Wellington are particularly useful because they write about doing research in education (although not specifically in FE or vocational training); and because their books are aimed at teachers doing research as part of their professional practice and CPD.

Opie, C. (2004) *Doing Educational Research.* London: Sage.
Wellington, J. (2000) *Educational Research: Contemporary Issues and Practical Approaches.* London: Continuum Press.
Yin, R. (2009) *Case Study Research: Design and Methods* (Fourth edition). London: Sage.

2
Research ethics and how we apply them in further education and training

The objectives of this chapter

This chapter explains how the British Educational Research Association (BERA) ethical guidelines should be applied in the context of Further and Adult Education, and is designed to help you to identify and work within the specific guidelines which are relevant to your own research. It provides definitions of what are meant by: *informed consent; confidentiality; vulnerable groups;* and *anonymity;* and discusses ways in which you can apply the principles embedded in this terminology to your own research.

Introduction

Before we go any further it is important that we understand why ethics – which we think of mainly as an important branch of philosophy – are so central to the conduct of educational research. So central, in fact, that we are discussing them now, in one of the earliest chapters, rather than bolting them on at the end. Part of the answer to this lies in the fact that every profession has its own code of ethical conduct, and teaching (which includes the reflection on practice which sometimes takes the form of formal research) is no exception. Usually, this requirement for ethical conduct can be summarised as 'do no harm'. Of course, for the medical profession the implications in terms of patient care are clear; and for the legal profession it is evidently about probity and integrity. But what does it mean for the teacher-researcher? Well, perhaps we can best express this as the requirement never to use our learners as simply a means to an end. This is a concept we associate with the philosopher, Immanuel Kant (1724–1804), who argued that all rational human beings should be treated as an end-in-themselves, and never as a means to something else. In other words, we do not have the right to *use* people for our own purposes. This important idea is central to Kant's moral philosophy and is sometimes referred to as his 'categorical imperative' – an essential and unassailable truth. Taken from our point of view as researchers it reminds us that we should not think of those we involve in the research as 'subjects' or 'objects' to be used for our own ends, but as *participants* who participate because they choose to, in secure knowledge of what this will involve. In other words, we must ensure that they are taking part in the research willingly and are fully aware of its purpose; that they are free to say, 'No' if they don't wish to participate; and that they understand that they have the right to withdraw from the research at any time. What this means in practice is that educational research should be conducted as a collaborative endeavour, with all participants having given their *informed consent*.

Little Albert and the rat

The other part of the answer as to why ethics should now be considered as so central to the conduct of research is the rather dark history of some aspects of research where, as recently as the twentieth century, people have been subjected without their knowledge, or even against their will, to various experiments whose so-called 'justification' was the advancement of knowledge. One of the more notorious cases is the experiment on 'Little Albert' by John Watson (1878–1958), an American psychologist and major figure in the development of the Behaviourist theory of learning. The experiment involved teaching an 11-month-old child, 'Little Albert', to learn to be afraid of a white rat. When first shown the rat the child showed no fear. He was then shown it again on several occasions, each time the appearance of the rat being accompanied by a loud noise. He learnt to associate the rat with the startling noise so that eventually he became conditioned to fear the rat, even when there was no noise involved. It seems that he was never 'un-conditioned'; and therefore the learnt fear remained a permanent part of his psychological makeup.

The Milgram experiment

Another well-known example of research that seems cruel to us now is what's come to be known as the Milgram experiment, in which 'participants' were induced to deliver what they believed were electric shocks of increasing painfulness as punishment for incorrect answers to 'learners' who were, unbeknown to them, played by actors. The researcher, Stanley Milgram, an American psychologist, began this research project in 1961 in order to measure people's willingness to obey orders from an authority figure – in the case of this experiment played by another actor in a white coat posing as a researcher. The hapless participants, who had responded to an advertisement offering an hourly rate of $4 to volunteers, were deceived on a number of counts: the purpose of the experiment, which they were told was about encouraging learning by punishing incorrect answers; the identities of others involved; the fiction that the 'electric shocks' they were administering were real; and that so were the sounds of pain and panic from behind the screen (which were, in fact, pre-recorded, again by actors). From our twenty-first-century perspective we can see how both of these research projects could – and probably did – inflict psychological and emotional damage on those who were subjected to them. To guard against any further such practices in the name of research there is fortunately now a requirement for researchers to adhere to ethical standards across all the sciences, including the social sciences, of which Education is one. For us these are set out clearly as a set of guidelines on the website of the British Educational Research Association (www.bera.ac.uk) and it is to these ethical standards that we shall be referring in this chapter and throughout the book.

TASK TASK **TASK** TASK **TASK TASK** TASK **TASK** TASK **TASK TASK** TASK

Now read the account of Jane Elliot's experiment below and consider the following questions:

- **In what ways does Elliot's experiment differ from those of Watson and Milgram in terms of the ethical issues raised?**

- **In what ways might we say it was similar?**

- **From your own personal point of view, is your sympathy with Elliot's critics or with Elliot herself, and why?**

- **To what extent do you believe that a positive motive or intent can justify a research method which may otherwise be ethically questionable?**

Blue eyes – brown eyes

In 1968 an American teacher and anti-racist activist, Jane Elliot (b.1933), conducted an experiment with her class of white eight-year-old pupils to discover whether she could develop their understanding of the implications of racism and prejudice. She had noted, from certain comments these children had been making about race and ethnicity, that they seemed to be accepting without question the racist attitudes prevalent amongst some white Americans at that time. She asked the class, therefore, whether they would like to try an experiment which would help them to understand what racism felt like. According to Elliott, the class agreed to this. She then divided the class according to eye colour. Those with blue eyes were the privileged group, entitled to extra helpings at lunch, extra playtime and seats at the front of the class. Those with brown eyes were given brown collars to make them more easily identifiable and were made to sit at the back of the class, allowed no privileges, forbidden to use the same drinking fountain as the blue-eyed group. Thus both groups were able to experience, from the inside, the power relationships and injustices which result from prejudice and discrimination. Elliot's experiment was greeted by some as an excellent exercise for diversity training, but condemned by others on ethical grounds. It continues to generate controversy to this day.

Discussion

Let's take those questions one by one.

- **First of all, does Elliot's experiment differ from those of Watson and Milgram in terms of ethics? You'll have noted that Elliott first asked her class whether they would like to try this activity, and explained its purpose. If this is the case, and they were all in agreement, then we could say that they have given their *informed consent*, which is certainly not the case for those subjected to Watson's and Milgram's research. Elliot's pupils, we are told, took part in the experiment by choice, and were therefore *participants* rather than simply subjects. However, there are two problems here. One is about power. The teacher is always in an implicit, even if not explicit, position of power in relation to those she teaches. It could be argued, therefore, that when she asks the class whether they would like to try the experiment there is an unspoken pressure on them to agree. This question of *power relations* is a very important one for us as teacher-researchers. We need to be aware of it not only when seeking participation or permission from our learners, but also when we are asking them questions as part of our research, because the power relationship between us may be experienced by them as a pressure to do or say what they think will please or impress us. (Although I'm sure at this point some of you are saying, 'I wish!')**

  The other problem here from an ethical point of view is the participants' age. To what extent can eight-year-olds be said to give *informed* consent? If you have already taken the opportunity to have a look online at the BERA ethical guidelines you will have seen references there to *vulnerable groups*. According to the guidelines, children under the age of 18 constitute one such group. Others, of equal relevance to those of us researching in FE, are people with learning difficulties, the over-70s and pregnant women. Some may take exception to the inclusion of these last two groups in the 'vulnerable' category, but we must remember that ethical guidelines must cover all types of research and experimentation activity, including those requiring participants to engage in activities which may be physically demanding or require disruption in diet or routine. When carrying out research with vulnerable groups the onus is on the researcher to ensure that the vulnerability is recognised and that safeguards are built into the research design and processes. In the case of research involving young children these days it would be required practice to obtain informed consent from parents or carers. This was not the case with Elliot's research.

- Therefore, in considering whether her experiment had similar ethical flaws to those of Watson and Milgram, we would have to say that, like them, she did not have what we would define today as *informed* consent. They did not have it because they did not seek it; she did not have it in any real sense because her participants were too young, according to modern guidelines, to give it in any meaningful way. It may also be the case that, like those earlier experiments, Elliot's may have caused its participants distress both at the time and possibly subsequently.

- So, is your sympathy with Elliot's critics or with Elliot herself? This is a difficult one, and it demonstrates that sometimes our own moral compass or confidence in our own integrity may be at odds with the strict ethical guidelines that we're required to follow. But, of course, that's exactly why the guidelines are there and why we need them. It is certainly difficult to disagree with Elliot's motives in wanting to raise the children's awareness of the effects of racism and discrimination. And this, of course, brings us on to the next point:

- Can a positive motive or intention ever justify a research method or design which may otherwise be ethically questionable? To answer this we need only to go back to Kant's categorical imperative, which reminds us that it is never justifiable to use people, even as a means to the most virtuous or noble ends.

CLOSE FOCUS CLOSE FOCUS CLOSE FOCUS CLOSE FOCUS CLOSE FOCUS

1. Read carefully the ethical research guidelines on the BERA website (www.bera.ac.uk) and identify at least three which are relevant to the research by: a) Watson and b) Milgram, which we looked at earlier.

2. Make a note of any points in the guidelines which you think may be particularly useful for you to refer to when carrying out your research in FE.

Let's have a look now at how some of these issues we've discussed might arise for a teacher carrying out a research project in the context of FE – and specifically in a general FE college.

TASK TASK TASK TASK TASK TASK TASK TASK TASK TASK TASK

As you read the account of Sean's experience below, consider the following questions. You'll find it useful to make a few notes so that you can compare your ideas and conclusions with those set out in the discussion which follows.

- What do you think are the ethical 'complications' which Sean's mentor warns him might arise if Sean decides to carry out individual interviews with the learners?

- In what way or ways would the use of anonymous questionnaires be a sounder option in terms of ethics?

- Sean seeks consent initially from his learners. Can their consent be taken as valid, given that they are under the age of 18 and therefore classed as a 'vulnerable group'?

- We're told that Sean plans to *get in under the class's radar*. What are the ethical implications of this?

- What are the strengths of a focus group approach, in terms of research ethics?

- What are the implications of seeking consent from parents or carers of minors, and not the minors themselves?

- What is Sean to do with the data from the discussion which included learners who had not given consent to be participants?

The tale of Sean and the unenthusiastic learners

Sean is in his first year of teaching Business Studies at a general FE college whose main campus is located in the centre of a large city. He has a degree in Business Administration and has worked for some years in a local firm before deciding to become a teacher and pass on his skills and enthusiasm to a new generation. The trouble is that this year his level 2 group of 16–18-year-olds is showing no enthusiasm at all, and their lack of engagement and couldn't-care-less attitude are beginning to get Sean down. He finds himself wondering why these learners have chosen to be on a Business Studies course at all if they are so obviously uninterested and can't be bothered to work at it. He discusses this with his mentor who suggests that Sean carries out some research to discover the answer to this question. This seems like a good idea, so Sean goes away a bit happier and starts designing a research project.

His initial idea is to interview the learners individually and ask them why they chose a Business Studies course and what they hoped to get out of it. However, his mentor points out that these learners, because of their age, constitute a vulnerable group and therefore one-to-one interviews with them would raise complications in terms of research ethics. She also reminds Sean that he will need to gain their consent before involving these learners as participants; and she advises him to have a look at the ethical guidelines for educational research on the BERA website. So Sean reads these through carefully and has a re-think and decides to use anonymous questionnaires to get his data. At the beginning of his next session with the group he explains to them that he wants to find out how and why they are taking this course and that he is going to give them a questionnaire in class which he'd like them to complete as honestly as possible. Bearing in mind the need for informed consent, he then points out to the learners that they are not obliged to do the questionnaire if they don't want to. Unfortunately – and he should perhaps have seen this coming – the entire class whoops with glee and declines to participate in the research.

Determined that there must be a way to do this, Sean has another chat with his mentor. This time they come up with the idea of holding a class discussion in the form of a focus group. Sean has been explaining to the learners about focus groups in relation to marketing and advertising, and so he hopes that by using this format to obtain the data he needs he will be able to slip his research questions in under the class's radar. He plans to tell them they will be acting as a focus group to explore the reasons why people might choose to go to an FE college to take a Business Studies course. To solve the problem of consent he decides to seek permission from their parents or carers for the learners to take part. To ensure that this is not simply consent but *informed* consent, he drafts a letter explaining his reasons for undertaking this research, and includes a reply slip for parents and carers to sign and return, stating that they understand the purpose of the research and give permission for the young person they are responsible for to take part in the focus group. Of the 19 letters he sends out, only three consent slips are returned. He has no way of knowing whether or not the non-returns represent consent withheld, but – feeling increasingly frustrated – he decides to go ahead with a focus group of just the three learners. The remainder are asked to be observers and to take notes.

The question he puts to the three participants is: 'Why should a school leaver choose to enrol on a level 2 Business Studies programme in FE?' At first the three give individual reasons, one saying her mum told her to do it; another that the school wouldn't keep him on because of poor results at the end of Year 11; the third that she wanted to go on *Dragons' Den*. But gradually the 'audience' becomes drawn in to the discussion and some very useful data begins to emerge. It seems that several of the class had assumed that Business Studies would be designed to develop their entrepreneurial skills and help them to get rich quick. Several more had enrolled only as a second choice, and would have preferred to have stayed on at school and studied A levels if the school had allowed them to. Three or four of the learners express a real interest in the subject, but complain that others in the group, who don't take it seriously, are spoiling their learning experience. Sean has been busy taking notes. At the end of the discussion he thanks them all and moves on to the next part of the lesson plan. But the discussion has given him some useful ideas. He writes up his notes that evening and decides he has the makings of a promising research paper. Clearly what he needs to do is to play up the entrepreneurial aspects of the modules wherever possible. This should engage the interest of the 'get rich quick' group, and perhaps make the subject more exciting for the 'second choice group'. So, he thinks, if he can get those two disaffected groups on task and on side, the learners with a genuine interest in the subject will be able to enjoy the lessons as they hoped to. All's well that ends well, it seems.

However, when Sean shows his mentor the first draft of his research paper explaining how he gathered his data, she tells him she's worried that he still doesn't seem to have grasped the importance or purpose of following ethical guidelines. We'll be exploring some of her concerns in the discussion that follows.

Discussion

We might imagine, judging from Sean's experience, that applying research ethics is a difficult or complicated process. But this is not at all the case. Sean's problems arise from the fact that he hasn't used the ethical guidelines as a starting point when designing his research project, but instead has tried to 'fit in' the ethical considerations afterwards. You'll be asked shortly to think about how you would go about applying the more sensible, ethics-based approach; but first let's look at those questions we raised at the beginning of the task, and – in the process – explore some of the ethical problems which are worrying Sean's mentor.

1. So, what do you think are the ethical 'complications' arising from individual interviews and which Sean's mentor warns him about?
- **One of the things which may have sprung to mind here is the power relationship between Sean and individual learners, which would be apparent in a one-to-one interview. As teacher, Sean is in a position of authority (even if it doesn't always feel like that!). How can he be sure, then, that the interviewee will not feel intimidated into giving answers designed to please or placate the teacher? This would not only call into question the *reliability* of the data obtained, but could also be seen as an abuse of power. In choosing to take a one-to-one interview approach, Sean could be accused of trying to elicit the answers he wants.**
- **Another potential problem which could arise from his choosing to conduct one-to-one interviews with younger learners is that Sean could leave himself open to untrue accusations of misconduct, unless he arranges for the interviews to be conducted in the presence of a witness or witnesses.**
- **There is also a difficulty here over the question of anonymity, particularly as their age categorises these learners as a vulnerable group. Sean must pay due attention to the need for safeguarding these young learners and ensuring that they, their views and their stories cannot be identified. The use of interviews, as with any method which involves participants on an individual rather than group basis, makes safeguarding anonymity much more difficult than – say – the use of focus groups, where responses are not attributed to individuals but to the collective voice of the group.**

2. In what way or ways did you think that the use of anonymous questionnaires would be a sounder option in terms of ethics?
- **First of all it's clear that anonymity addresses to a large extent the problem of the power imbalance inherent in teacher-learner interactions. Sean won't know whose answers are whose, and so learners should feel less pressure to say the 'right' thing.**
- **Second, he won't have to be alone with individuals on a one-to-one basis. This means that they won't feel intimidated and that he won't leave himself vulnerable to untrue allegations of any kind.**

3. When Sean seeks consent initially from his learners, should he take their consent as valid, given that their age classifies them as a vulnerable group?

- **This is a very interesting question, and one which you may find useful to discuss further with a colleague or mentor. The important point here is the need for the researcher to find a balance between disempowering a vulnerable group by asking someone else to make their decision for them, or treating them with respect as potential participants who have the right to make the decision themselves. In the end it probably comes down to whether the researcher can be confident that consent is given or withheld on the basis of a clear understanding of what is involved. This is what we mean, of course, by *informed* consent.**

- **If you think back to Watson's research which we discussed early in this chapter you will probably be of the view that Little Albert, at 11 months old, would be incapable of giving informed consent. In his case, it would be proper for consent to be sought from his parent or guardian (though it seems astonishing to us now that such consent was given). Sean's group of young adults were probably perfectly capable of giving informed consent. The fact that Sean decided, when they did not, to ask their parents instead, is arguably his worst breach of research ethics.**

- **The whole question of consent leads us also, of course, to questions about agency, advocacy, empowerment and disempowerment which are central to our practice as teachers as well as researchers.**

4. So what are the ethical implications of Sean's plans to *'get in under the class's radar'*?

- **Ethically, this is very bad practice. Participants should, by definition, be aware of what they are participating in, and why. What Sean proposes is a kind of deceit. If you have not seen these already, have a look at what the BERA guidelines have to say about practising deceit on research participants (www.bera.ac.uk).**

5. What do you think are the strengths of a focus group approach, in terms of research ethics?

- **As we discussed in answer to question 1 above, focus groups are useful when seeking data from vulnerable groups because individuals are neither indentified nor identifiable.**

- **The data collected is more reliable because it doesn't rely on one individual's viewpoint, and is less open to influence by the researcher.**

- **Speaking through the collective voice of the focus group is of benefit for younger participants. The experience may feel less intimidating than an interview; and the strength in numbers to some extent counters the power imbalance implicit in teacher-learner interactions.**

6. What are the implications of seeking consent from parents or carers of minors, and not the minors themselves? Well, we've addressed this to some extent in answering question 3. But it's interesting to reflect on a couple of further points here:

- **What if the parent agrees to give consent but the learner *dis*agrees? What's the ethical position then? Or what if that position were reversed?**

- **To obtain consent the researcher usually must give a guarantee of *confidentiality*. This is different from anonymity, which is about protecting the identity of the participant, the institution, other individuals mentioned in the data, and who said what. Confidentiality is about who is allowed to see the responses or data provided by the participant. The ethical question to reflect on here is whether parents who have given consent should have the right to see what the learner has said.**

7. What is Sean to do with the data from the discussion which included learners who had not given consent to be participants?

* **This is another very tricky one. Sean might argue that, by deciding to contribute to the discussion, they were implicitly, if belatedly, giving their consent. Would you agree with that?**
* **Or perhaps he could check with them afterwards to discover whether they would have any objection to his taking as part of his data the parts of the discussion in which they were involved.**

CLOSE FOCUS CLOSE FOCUS CLOSE FOCUS CLOSE FOCUS CLOSE FOCUS

Poor Sean! He seems to have had one problem after another. But there was no need for it to be like that. Reflecting on his various decisions and mistakes, and with the benefit of hindsight, think about how *you* would have gone about designing this research and how you would have addressed the issue of informed consent.

A SUMMARY OF **KEY POINTS**

In this chapter we have looked at the importance of following ethical guidelines for research, and seen how they encourage and remind us to:

> think carefully about how we manage the power relationship between ourselves and our participants;

> ensure that participants understand the purpose of the research and their role within it;

> inform participants that they have the right to withdraw from the research at any time;

> check whether any or all of our participants may be defined as belonging to a vulnerable group, and ensure that our research is designed to take account of that vulnerability where necessary;

> design research which does not set out to use people for our own ends;

> where appropriate, ask participants to check for accuracy the wording of anything you have quoted them as saying, and obtain their approval for using that quote;

> anonymise names of people, places and institutions in order to maintain confidentiality.

We have also identified some useful terms to use when talking about research ethics. These include: *informed consent; confidentiality; vulnerable groups; anonymity; participants; power relationship; Kant's categorical imperative.*

Branching options

You may like to choose one of the following activities which are designed to help you apply what you've learnt from this chapter to your own practice. The first encourages you, as a professional, to develop your skills of reflection; the second asks you to take an evaluative approach consistent with an initial teaching qualification in the sector; and the third is designed to support skills of critical analysis appropriate to post-qualification CPD or Masters level study.

Reflection

Imagine that you intend to carry out a piece of research along the same lines as Sean's. Write one paragraph to explain how your research design will ensure that you are conforming to the BERA ethical guidelines.

Evaluation

Think of an aspect of your recent professional experience that you would like to research. Who would the participants be? What ethical issues might you need to take into account when deciding how to gather your data? How might your consideration of ethics influence the design of your research?

Critical analysis

Read through the following list of three examples and decide whether they do or do not conform to the ethical guidelines we have discussed in this chapter. Are there any you would describe as 'grey areas'? If you think so, it would be useful to discuss these with a tutor, colleague or mentor.

1. A teacher-researcher plans to conduct one-to-one interviews with a small group of adult learners whom she does not personally teach. Will this raise any ethical issues?

2. Being short of time, a teacher-researcher decides that, instead of giving out questionnaires to his class to find out what they topics and methods they have enjoyed most, he will use instead learner evaluation forms on which his class has given feedback about their most recent module. As these have already been completed, does he need to ask the learners' consent to use them as research data?

3. A teacher-researcher wants to know whether parental attitudes have an influence on learners' behaviour. She decides to question her class about their parents' attitudes to education in general and the college in particular. Does this raise ethical questions? And if so, what are they?

FURTHER READING   FURTHER READING   FURTHER READING   FURTHER READING

The following two books explore in detail the ethical issues we've been looking at in this chapter. Sikes et al. (2003) is an edited collection of chapters by various authors, which provide a very thorough account of ethics as they relate to Educational research. The term used by the editors is 'moral' rather than 'ethical'; and you might find it interesting to consider what the distinction is, if any. If you can't find the time to read the entire book you could usefully focus on Chapter 3, written by Sikes and Goodson and entitled: 'Living research: thoughts on educational research as moral practice'. The book by Alderson and Morrow (2011), while not specifically written for teachers, is excellent in dealing with the problems of researching with participants from vulnerable groups such as young people, and provides insight into some of the important current debates and legal issues.

Alderson, P. and Morrow, V. (2011) *The Ethics of Research with Children and Young People*. London: Sage.

Sikes, P., Nixon, J. and Carr, W. (eds) (2003) *The Moral Foundations of Educational Research: Knowledge, Inquiry and Values*. Maidenhead: Open University Press.

3
Choosing and planning your research project

The objectives of this chapter

The purpose of this chapter is to help you to review your own professional interests and experiences in order to find a focus for your project. It includes 'real life' vignettes showing examples of how teachers and student teachers have chosen a topic for research, and how they have gone about planning practicable and realistic ways to approach it. At the same time it provides guidance on how to formulate your research question in the most useful way, and how to recognise the limitations of an inquiry as well as its relevance to your own teaching and learning. In this way it continues to explore the concept of research as integral to professional practice and provides definitions of what is meant by: *action research; research journal; scale and scope; research question; research aims; transferability; generalisability*.

Introduction

This chapter is all about choosing and formulating your research question. Before we have a look at examples of how other teachers in FE and vocational training have approached this, it's important to note that there are four key considerations when evaluating a topic or focus for research. These are: *relevance; scale; feasibility* or *access;* and the wording of your *title.*

Relevance

For teachers, the purpose of undertaking educational research is usually to help us to gain a better understanding of some aspect or topic relating to our own professional practice. Our research is carried out with a view to developing our professional range and confidence and – directly or indirectly – improving the learning experience of those we teach. For these reasons the first requirement when choosing a research topic is *relevance*: to our current work and future aspirations; to the needs of our learners; and to our own particular area of interest or enthusiasm. This last point is an important one and essential to your motivation as a researcher. A teacher's life is a busy one, particularly in FE; and to take on a research project on top of those everyday demands on your time requires stamina and commitment. If the focus of your research is something that genuinely engages your interest, this will be a great advantage.

Scale

As well as relevance, you will also have to consider the matter of *scale.* Your chosen topic must be *manageable* within the time and resources available. It is one thing to investigate the previous educational experiences of one group of adult learners on an Access course; but quite another to try and survey those experiences nationally. First-time researchers sometimes express concern that very small-scale research, focused on just one group of learners for example, is not really 'proper' research at all. But if the researcher's aim is to discover something about that specific group, something that will help them to improve the group's experience of learning for example, then of course it can justifiably be called research. But if, on the other hand, the researcher attempts to *generalise* from that data and claim that the findings are applicable to all groups of adult learners everywhere, then plainly that is a nonsense and we can't take it seriously as research at all. If you want to discover something related to the learners you teach, or the institution you work in, then make these the focus of your inquiry and the subject to which you apply your findings. Smallness of scale only becomes a problem if you start making claims that suggest your findings are transferable or generalisable to other groups or contexts. You may have a professional interest in whether your findings might apply more widely, and it's perfectly all right to express this interest as a question when, for example, you are writing up the conclusion to your research project. This may well encourage other researchers to discover whether their own research within their specific working context will arrive at the same findings.

Feasibility and access

A third important consideration when choosing your research topic is *feasibility*. Are you attempting the impossible? Can you gain *access* to the people or the information you need? Have you chosen a research question to which it is realistic to seek an answer? For example, if you were thinking of pursuing the question of why government policy imposes such frequent changes on the further education sector you would almost certainly be setting yourself an impossible task. Government ministers might be an obvious source of data, but it's not certain that you would gain access to interview them. And, even if you did so, could you justifiably take one minister's response as the definitive answer to your question? On the other hand, if you were to approach your chosen topic from a different angle and investigate, for example, the *impact* of a recent policy change on the working practices of one department in your institution, you would have a *manageable* research project, feasible in terms of time and scale, and – presumably – presenting no problems of access.

Choosing a title

Your choice of a title for your research project is not only about giving a clear indication to others of the topic and the context of your inquiry; it is also a means of keeping you on track and sharply focused as you carry out and then write up your research. That's why it's useful to make the title and the research question one and the same, and to word it with precision. It will then act not only as a useful 'signpost' to anyone reading the research, but also as a reassuring compass for you, the researcher, reminding you of what is and what is not relevant to your purpose as you navigate your way through all the literature and the data. Adding a subtitle to your title-as-research-question can also further clarify the context and the scale of the research. For example, compare these two titles:

'Supporting learners with dyslexia.'

and

'What strategies are most effective in supporting the written language skills of level 2 hospitality and catering students with dyslexia? A study in one West Midlands FE college.'

Note here how, in the second title, the researcher has clearly identified the specific nature of the inquiry in terms of the question and the students, as well as the level and vocational area. The addition of the subtitle (the section after the question mark) gives us additional useful information about the scale or extent of the inquiry. If we saw a paper with this title in a research journal or online we would be able to see immediately whether or not it was relevant to our own work. This clarity in the wording of your title is what you should always aim for; and in the next two sections we shall see some further examples of teachers formulating research questions as titles which accurately express the purpose, scale and context of their inquiry.

TASK TASK **TASK** TASK **TASK TASK** TASK **TASK** TASK **TASK TASK** TASK

Raj, Di and Hamish all teach at the same large FE College and are all undertaking research projects as part of their professional development. On the advice of their tutor they have decided to meet for half an hour once a week as a critical friendship group, to discuss their individual projects and share advice and support. For their first meeting their tutor joins them to make sure they are all on the right track and are not planning research that might prove to be unmanageable or doomed to failure in some other way.

You can eavesdrop on their meeting by reading through the dialogue below. Read it carefully, and make notes of any key points which you think will help you in your own research. Following the dialogue you will find a series of questions, which invite you to reflect on the key points which this meeting raised.

Tutor: Let's start by hearing about your research questions. Di, do you want to go first?

Di: Okay. Well, I've got to do something with my level 2 beauty therapists. They've no idea how to talk to clients. If you tell them to make conversation they just clam up. And if they do say anything, they can't seem to understand the difference between the language you'd use with a client in a work situation and the way you'd talk to your mates on a night out. Effing this and effing that. So I want to try some different ways of developing their communication skills so I can find out what works. Trouble is, I'm not sure that's really what you'd call research, is it?

Tutor: Well, is it? What do we think?

Raj: Isn't that what you call *action research*?

Tutor: Absolutely! Spot on! It's a very good example of an action research model, in fact. Can you tell us what it is that makes it action research, then, Raj?

Raj: It's because she's researching her own practice – her own teaching – so that she can find out what works. It's like a sort of experiment.

Tutor: Exactly. In action research you identify something you want to change – in your case, Di, it's the learners' poor communication skills – and then you make what are called 'interventions', changes to the style or content of your teaching, for example. And then you look again and see whether you've succeeded in bringing about the change you intended. It's a cycle: identify the issue; make the intervention; check the result; if you've not succeeded in bringing about the desired change, make a different intervention; and so on...

Hamish: So something on as small a scale as that can be called research? Just focusing on your own teaching?

Tutor: Yes, indeed. Because – let's face it – for most teachers, what research could be more valuable and more relevant to their own professional practice than an evaluation of that practice itself?

Hamish: Aye, well, in that case I reckon I'm going to feel free to scale mine down a bit, you know.

Raj: What were you intending to do, then?

Hamish: Well, I *was* intending to try and find out why so many people think it's smarter to study A levels in a sixth form than a level 3 qualification in FE.

Di: Wow.

Raj: So no pressure there then.

Tutor: How were you proposing to find an answer to that, Hamish?

Hamish: Asking people, I suppose.

Tutor: What people?

Hamish: Aye, well, you've got me there, I'm afraid.

Di: People would have different views, though, wouldn't they, depending on who you ask? School heads would probably say it was because schools offer a better option and A levels get you further in life, that sort of thing. But people teaching in FE would probably say it was down to snobbery or bad press...

Raj: Or career advisors' prejudice. And historians would say it was all down to eighteenth-century ideas about education for gentlemen...

Di: So how would you decide which was the right answer? Or whether it was something else, or a combination. And you'd be deciding *who* to ask and who to believe, so your own bias would be built in from the start.

Tutor: And it's a very *big* question, isn't it, Hamish? And one that almost certainly has a very complex answer. It would be pretty big, even as a PhD topic. And the way you've phrased it: '*Why* so many people think that...etc.; etc.' It suggests you're going to be surveying the entire population over the age of 16.

Hamish: Okay! Okay! It's rubbish. I get it.

Tutor: No, no. Not rubbish at all. A very interesting question, in fact. But one that you just don't have the time or resources to tackle for the purpose of this project. So let's see if we can scale it down a bit, find a way to address the same topic but in a manageable way. Anyone any ideas?

Di: What if he just focused on one of his classes, like I'm doing? What if he just asked them why they think...

Hamish: Hang on, though. I think it's not just the scale. It's the way I'm phrasing the question, isn't it? So what if I focused on my own learners, like Di said, and asked them a question they could give a proper answer to – an answer that I could take as reasonably reliable. Like, 'What do you think are the advantages and disadvantages of taking a vocational course at college, compared to taking A levels in a school sixth form?'

Tutor: Good. That would work.

Raj: So your title and your research question could be something along the lines of : '*What do level 3 learners in FE consider to be the advantages and disadvantages of studying for a vocational qualification in an FE college rather than studying A levels in school?*'

Tutor: Yes, that's a good working title. Involving level 3 learners gives you a direct comparison with A level. And focusing on your own learners means that your findings will be helpful and relevant to your own teaching. Knowing what learners value about their course, and why they chose it, are always useful when you're looking for ways to keep up their motivation. But you'll have to tweak that title a bit so that the scale and scope of your inquiry are clear.

Hamish: Yes, thanks Raj. I owe you one. So tell us about yours.

Raj: Okay, well I teach accountancy, right? So you won't be surprised that I'm thinking of doing something that involves a bit of number crunching.

Hamish: Quantitative analysis.

Raj: Right. I'm going to stick to numbers because I don't think my question is the sort of thing that need involve collecting people's opinions or experiences or anything like that. Basically what I want to find out is whether the attainment results for students who live a long distance from the college are over all better or worse than – or the same as – the results of students who have a very short distance to travel.

Di: Why?

Raj: Well, I've got this theory, you see, that the ones who have to travel a long distance to get in are possibly more committed, on the whole, than those who live only around the corner and may be coming here just because it's easier for them than going somewhere else. For example, if someone wants to study accountancy in this county they have to come to this college because nowhere else offers it. If they weren't that serious about the subject they'd probably just think to hell with it and choose a different course at a college nearer home. Do you see where I'm coming from?

Tutor: So how would you obtain your data about distance travelled?

Raj: I'd just look at postcodes. And then I'd do a straight comparison – which could be set out as a graph – of distance travelled and attainment scores. It'd be easy to see straight away if there was any correlation.

Tutor: Okay. And how would you be able to apply your findings? Let's assume for a minute that your theory turns out to be supported by your data; what then? How would that discovery be useful to you?

Raj: I guess it would help me to understand the motivation of my learners a bit better?

We'll leave the meeting at that point in order to consider the following questions, answers to which are suggested in the discussion below:

1. We haven't discovered how Di's research title will be worded. What wording, in your view, would best express her aims and scope?
2. When Di says to Hamish, 'And you'd be deciding *who* to ask and who to believe, so your own bias would be built in from the start,' Hamish might easily have replied, 'Well, how is that different from what you're proposing to do? Your research focuses entirely on you, so that must build in bias, mustn't it?' Why do you think concerns are voiced about bias in Hamish's initial proposal, but not about Di's action research?
3. The tutor tells Hamish that he will have to 'tweak' his title a bit to make the scale and scope of his inquiry clear. What 'tweaks' would you advise?
4. Raj says of his research method: 'I'd just look at postcodes. And then I'd do a straight comparison – which could be set out as a graph – of distance travelled and attainment scores. It'd be easy to see straight away if there was any correlation.' a) What does he mean by the word 'correlation' here, and why is it a very useful one for researchers? b) Thinking back to the previous chapter, would Raj be required to obtain informed consent from the learners whose postcodes he was looking up?

Discussion

1. To keep her focused and to convey to others the precise nature of her research, Di's title will need to include clearly: a) her question; b) the scope and scale of her inquiry; and c) her approach (in this case, action research). It would therefore look something like this: *'What strategy is most effective for developing the spoken communication skills of level 2 learners on a beauty therapy programme at one large FE college: An action research inquiry'*. We can identify the three components of the title more

clearly when we set them out like this:

a)	Her basic question:	'What strategy is most effective for developing the spoken communication skills ...
b)	The scope and scale of her inquiry:	'...of level 2 learners on a beauty therapy programme at one large FE college:
c)	Her approach:	'An action research inquiry.'

2. So, why *do* you think concerns are voiced about bias in Hamish's initial proposal, but not about Di's action research? The answer is that the vulnerability to bias that is inherent in Hamish's plan for data gathering is unacknowledged in his research question. He will be choosing whom to question, based on his own preconceptions of who can provide him with answers; and the responses of those participants will be shaped in turn by their own values and beliefs. In what sense, therefore, can those responses be regarded as constituting an objective 'truth'? But these layers of subjectivity are not apparent in his title, which masquerades as an objective, 'factual' inquiry. Di's title, on the other hand, is quite explicit about the researcher and her professional concerns being at the centre of her inquiry. This is action research, and so that is where she needs to be. Her research is about her practice and about which teaching and learning strategies work best for her and her learners. Subjectivity is necessary here. In fact, it is accepted practice for action researchers to incorporate extracts from their own reflective journals into the writing up of their research, as we shall see in more detail in Chapter 4.

3. Hamish's revised title currently reads like this:

    'What do level 3 learners in FE consider to be the advantages and disadvantages of studying for a vocational qualification in an FE college rather than studying A levels in school?'

    We now need to consider what additions or changes he would need to make in order to indicate the scale of his inquiry, as the tutor suggests. Remember, the proposed scope of his original research idea was unfeasible and unmanageable, so it's important that he gets the wording of this revised version right. He could achieve this by simply adding a subtitle something like this:

    'A study based on data from one department of a large FE college.'

    Or he could incorporate this indication of scale into the wording of the title, like this:

    'What do level 3 learners in one department of a large FE college consider to be the advantages and disadvantages of studying for a vocational qualification in college rather than studying A levels in school?'

    Whichever of these two ways he does it, he will leave no room for misunderstandings about the scale of his inquiry.

4a. What Raj means by 'correlation' is a pattern or a match. For example, if learners with the highest attainment scores are those with postcodes furthest away from the college, we can say that there is a correlation between longer distances travelled into college and high levels of attainment. Similarly, if learners with poor attainment scores tend to have postcodes which locate them within walking distance of the college, we can say that there is a correlation between living in close proximity to the college and poor levels of attainment. What we *can't* claim is that this is a matter of cause and effect. We may have discovered that learners who live far from the college tend to get better results, but this doesn't necessarily mean that the one causes the other. We can't know that some other factor may be responsible. For example, there might be an excellent secondary school whose catchment lies at some distance from the college and which has produced potentially high attaining learners. The word 'correlation', therefore, is a very useful one for researchers as it allows us to draw attention to patterns or matches in our data and to speculate about them without being tempted to make unsupported claims about cause and effect.

4b. The simple answer to this question is that Raj would *not* need informed consent to look up learners' postcodes. Why? First of all because this is information which the college already holds on record; and second, because by the very nature of his research learners themselves will not be involved, either as individuals or as groups, nor even as postcodes! Raj is looking only to see whether there is a correlation between postcodes and attainment. Such correlation, or the lack of it, is the only data that will be presented.

CLOSE FOCUS CLOSE FOCUS **CLOSE FOCUS** CLOSE FOCUS **CLOSE FOCUS**

How would you advise Raj to word his research question, which he will also use as his title? (If you found it useful you could refer to the title set out in a table in the discussion of question 1.)
You might like to begin like this:
'Is there a correlation between. . . .'

A SUMMARY OF **KEY POINTS**

In this chapter we have discussed:
> **key considerations to bear in mind when choosing your research focus;**
> **the importance of articulating a precise and clearly worded research question which will also serve as a working title.**

We have also identified some useful terms to use when talking about formulating our research question. These include: *action research; research journal; scale and scope; research question; research aims; transferability; generalisability; relevance; manageability; feasibility; access; correlation.*

Branching options

You may like to choose one of the following activities which are designed to help you apply what you've learnt from this chapter to your own practice. The first encourages you, as a professional, to develop your skills of reflection; the second asks you to take an evaluative approach consistent with an initial teaching qualification in the sector; and the third is designed to support skills of critical analysis appropriate to post-qualification CPD or Masters level study.

Reflection

Siobhan is interested in finding out how the new exam system for Year 11 in schools might affect school leavers' choices locally. Will it affect the numbers choosing to enter the College of FE where she works as a department head? Will it have any impact on their choice of vocational subject? Siobhan has all the numerical data for the last three years, showing a general stability in student numbers progressing to the various departments of her college from local feeder schools. She wonders whether head teachers and teachers may be able to give her some indication of what impact the new arrangements might have on this stability as the first cohorts begin to feed through the new system. She decides to interview key staff in local schools about pupil aspirations and expectations, and comes up with the following research title: *'Expected patterns of progression from school to FE college.'*

What advice would you give Siobhan about this title? Re-draft it for her in a more useful and precise form which will be clear and helpful both to her and to her participants.

Evaluation

Evaluate the following draft research questions in terms of *feasibility, scope* and *relevance:*

- Richard is a sports science teacher. His draft question is: *'What impact did the 2012 Olympic Games have on the motivation of young UK athletes?'*
- Alia leads the Adult Basic Skills team. Her question is: *'What form of "reward" is most effective in motivating Adult Basic Skills learners? A case study in one North Eastern college.'*
- Modesty teaches ICT at level 3 and above. Her research question is: *'To what extent does the opportunity to use computers at an early age help the acquisition of ICT skills post-16?'*
- Darryl is a new appointment to college middle management and heads up the Built Environment team. He wants to research the following question: *'Are excellent rugby players usually those who have had the opportunity of rugby training at school?'*

Critical analysis

Let's look again at what was said in the critical friendship group about Hamish's plan to 'ask people' why A levels in the sixth form were widely considered a higher status option than a vocational course in FE.

Di: People would have different views, though, wouldn't they, depending on who you ask? School heads would probably say it was because schools offer a better option and A levels get you further in life, that sort of thing. But people teaching in FE would probably say it was down to snobbery or bad press. . .

Raj: Or career advisors' prejudice. And historians would say it was all down to eighteenth-century ideas about education for gentlemen. . .

Di: So how would you decide which was the right answer? Or whether it was something else, or a combination. And you'd be deciding who to ask and who to believe, so your own bias would be built in from the start.

Di and Raj seem to be suggesting here that people's views and opinions can't be taken as valuable or trustworthy data. However, they express no such objections to Hamish's revised question, which has now become: *'What do level 3 learners in FE consider to be the advantages and disadvantages of studying for a vocational qualification in an FE college rather than studying A levels in school?'*

i)   Why is this not regarded as presenting the same problems about reliability?
ii) Can you think of a way to reword Hamish's original research question so that using people's views and opinions as data would not raise questions about reliability or trustworthiness?

(We'll be revisiting these two questions in Chapter 5, where you'll be able to compare your own answer to the one provided there.)

FURTHER READING FURTHER READING FURTHER READING FURTHER READING

The following two books provide additional advice and examples. Atkins and Wallace (2012), although written for teachers in all sectors rather than specifically FE, has a useful first chapter, 'Research in Education', which looks in detail at how to formulate and refine your research question. Bell (2010) contains some simple, step-by-step advice for research projects in general.

Atkins, L. and Wallace, S. (2012) *Qualitative Research in Education*. London: Sage.
Bell, J. (2010) *Doing your Research Project: A Guide for First-time Researchers in Education, Health and Social Science*. Maidenhead: Open University Press.

4
Looking in the mirror:
Action Research as reflective practice

The objectives of this chapter

This chapter provides a clear explanation of what is (and what is not) meant by 'Action Research'. It looks at examples of the Action Research spiral in an FE context, and discusses the link between Action Research and reflective practice. It shows, by examples, how Action Research can be a valuable tool for the FE practitioner, and introduces the terminology associated with it, including: *action research cycle; action research spiral; intervention; reflective practice; reflective journal; living theory; critical theory action research; cycles of action; practitioner research; cyclical.*

Introduction

In the previous three chapters we have been following the essential stages of thinking and planning which the teacher-researcher must work through before making a start on the research itself. These stages are:

*   **recognising the relevance of research to the FE teacher's role, and the usefulness of undertaking it (Chapter 1);**
*   **considering the ethical implications of their intended research, and ensuring that their purpose and approach conform to the accepted ethical guidelines (Chapter 2);**
*   **arriving at a specific research question and wording it so as to accurately express the purpose, context and scale of their research (Chapter 3).**

This chapter, and the ones that follow, explore the various methods and approaches open to teachers who are carrying out research in an FE and vocational training context, so that you can select those which best suit your purpose. We're going to look at Action Research first, partly because its basic principles will be immediately recognisable to all reflective practitioners, which means we'll be starting with what is familiar; and partly because it is in many ways the most manageable in terms of your time, and yet potentially the most productive in terms of impact on your own professional practice.

We've already seen a brief explanation of what the term means in Chapter 3 when the tutor was talking to Di about her research idea. This is what he said:

> *'In action research you identify something you want to change – in your case, Di, it's the learners' poor communication skills – and then you make what are called "interventions", changes to the style or content of your teaching, for example. And then you look again and see whether you've succeeded in bringing about the change you intended. It's a cycle: identify the issue; make the intervention; check the result; if you've not succeeded in bringing about the desired change, make a different intervention; and so on..'*

This is quite a simplified explanation, and one which applies to a specific type of Action Research most closely related to what we usually think of as reflective practice. Raj sums this approach up well when he says: *'It's like a sort of experiment'.* And indeed it is. At its most basic level, it's about finding out what works to improve our professional practice, and what doesn't. The word 'Action' in the term *Action Research* reminds us of the two essential aspects of this sort of inquiry:

- It involves us *taking action* of some sort. We do something – we act – and then we observe and evaluate the results of that action.
- In this type of research, we are the *main actor,* the central character. The focus of the research is on our professional practice and on how our 'actions' impact on the learning experience of our students.

This process of such research is often represented as a cycle or a spiral. We could also picture it simply like this:

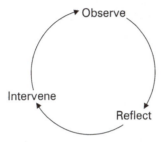

Figure 4.1: A simple reflective cycle

If we are not satisfied with our first intervention, our cycle can become a spiral as we go through the process again, this time with a greater understanding:

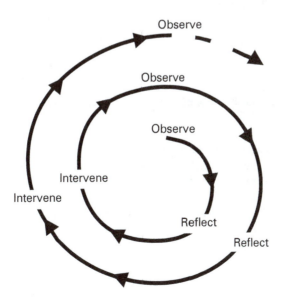

Figure 4.2: A double reflective cycle, or spiral

Dmitri tries some Action Research

To picture this in action (forgive the pun), let's imagine a Hospitality and Catering teacher – we'll call him Dmitri – who is having difficulties with his learners' lack of punctuality. Nothing he has tried so far has persuaded them to arrive on time, and this creates a serious problem for Dmitri because the timetable gives him a limited time for these practical lessons in the kitchen. If the learners turn up late he can't get through everything he needs to. A colleague suggests he tries introducing something the learners should find unmissable at the start of every lesson. Dmitri announces to his unpunctual group that next lesson he'll be offering them the demonstration cakes and pastries he'll have prepared in an earlier class, but it will be on a first-come-first-served basis. This inducement works quite well and next time most of the class arrives earlier than usual. So, has Dmitri done a bit of Action Research? Well, in a very instrumental way he has because he's learnt something from this experiment, which is that the learners will respond to the offer of a reward. He may need to pursue this a bit further in order to arrive at an effective reward which is a bit more pedagogically respectable than cake – but at least he's getting somewhere in terms of understanding learners' motivation and how he can use this to help them engage with their learning. So we can represent Dmitri's actions like this:

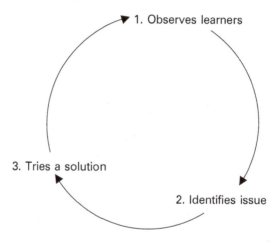

Figure 4.3: Dmitri's cycle of observation, intervention and reflection

He might decide to stick with the cakes; or he might try something else – make another intervention – such as giving all punctual learners the role of chef but relegating latecomers to the less prestigious role of assistant chefs, putting them at the beck and call of their more punctual peers on the grounds that those who arrive in time will have learned more about the task in hand. To discover whether this will induce punctuality he will need to go through another research cycle. When we represent this process diagrammatically, it begins to look like the spiral we saw on page 29.

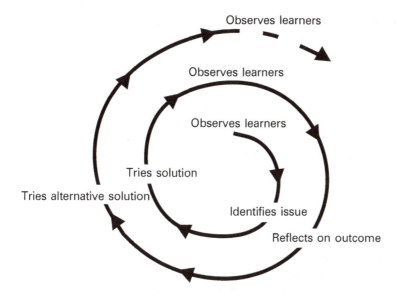

Observes learners

Observes learners

Observes learners

Tries solution

Tries alternative solution

Identifies issue

Reflects on outcome

Figure 4.4: Dmitri, on reflection, tries an alternative intervention

TASK TASK **TASK** TASK **TASK TASK** TASK **TASK** TASK **TASK TASK** TASK

Taking into account what we have discussed so far, consider the list of research projects below and decided which of these is Action Research, and why. You will probably find it useful to make some notes so that you can compare your answers to those in the discussion which follows.

- Annie wants to find out more about her students' learning styles so that she can ensure that her lesson planning takes account of the full range of styles in her level 3 Business Studies class.

- Bashir is having difficulties getting a small group of three girls to engage with his lessons. They always sit together, remain silent throughout the session and avoid making any eye-contact with him or with any others in the group. This makes formative assessment – for example, through whole group work or question and answer – difficult. The only way he can ascertain whether they are achieving the lesson objectives is through setting written work. He is worried that they are missing out on valuable learning experiences such as group discussion; and so he decides to keep trying out various strategies until he finds some way to draw them in without making them uncomfortable.

- Frankie, a part-time teacher, has noticed that the groups of 16–18-year-olds he teaches respond more positively to some teachers than to others. He wants to find out what it is that these 'successful' teachers do that keeps learners engaged. So he arranges to observe colleagues' classes in his own time.

- Clare has been told by her mentor that she tends to direct her eye contact towards the right hand side of the classroom, ignoring learners who sit on her left and therefore not noticing when they have a question or are off task. To see for herself whether this really is the case, she arranges to have three of her teaching sessions recorded so that she can see herself in action.

- Ernest is leader of the ICT team. One of his new colleagues, Bob, is really struggling with his lesson planning and his classroom management, although he keeps insisting that, 'Everything's all right'. As team leader and also as Bob's mentor, Ernest needs to find the best way to support this colleague who clearly doesn't want to admit that he needs help. So, first of all, Ernest suggests that they do a session of team teaching together. He hopes this will provide the opportunity for them to discuss the lesson afterwards. But Bob just sits back and lets Ernest do all the teaching. Not deterred, Ernest invites Bob to sit in on a couple of his lessons and then go for a coffee afterwards to talk about whether Bob's learnt anything useful. Bob observes, but skips the coffee and discussion. Ernest tries to think of what to try next.

- Zaneb teaches on a foundation degree programme. She notices that many of the students – all adults – are not confident about taking notes. She knows that they'll need note-taking skills if they are to succeed on their course and also if they choose to progress to a university, and so she decides to try out various ways of introducing note-taking into her lessons so as to find the most effective way of equipping her students with the skills they need.

Discussion

- Annie wants to find out more about her students' learning styles and will use this information to inform her lesson planning. So is this Action Research? You probably recognised that no, it's not. Her eventual aim may be to use her data to develop her own professional practice, but most research carried out by teachers has this aim in view. Annie is planning to collect data *about her learners*, and not about her own practice. She'll collect this data by – presumably – asking the learners to complete a questionnaire, not by observing or monitoring her own practice. There is no experiment involved here. She isn't planning to try a strategy or an intervention and reflect on the outcome. Her research will not be a cyclical process. Her approach is linear and can be presented like this:

Identify question → Collect data → Analyse data → Answer question

We can refer to this model as *practitioner research*.

We have now identified four key questions to ask ourselves when deciding whether an inquiry can be described accurately as Action Research:

1. Does the data collection focus on monitoring and reflecting on my own practice?

2. Does it involve experimentation or trying out strategies?

3. Is the process cyclical?

4. Is the ultimate purpose to improve the quality of the students' learning and/or my own professional practice or behaviour as it impacts on others?

If the answer to any of these is 'No', then what you are considering is probably not Action Research.

- What about Bashir and his project aimed at finding a way to draw the small group of 'silent' girls into participating in the lesson? We know that he's decided to try out various strategies until he finds some way to draw them in without making them uncomfortable. His research, therefore, fits the four descriptors for Action Research that we've just set out. He will focus on his own practice – the strategies that he will use and reflect upon; the process will be cyclical; and he will experiment to discover an effective way of supporting these learners. Therefore we can say that Bashir's project does take the form of Action Research.

- We turn now to Frankie, who wants to carry out observations to find out what 'successful' teachers do that keeps learners engaged. Certainly his findings may be useful for his own professional practice, but what he proposes does not conform to an Action Research model. First, he plans to observe the practice of colleagues in order to obtain the data he needs. His own practice is not the main focus here. Second, his research does not involve him in experimenting with his practice to see whether he can bring about improvement either in himself or his learners.

- Then we have Clare who has been told that she favours one side of the room and ignores the other. Does her arrangement to have her teaching sessions video-recorded constitute Action Research? Well, she'll be able to see herself in action, and she'll be focusing on her own 'performance' as a teacher, and possibly reflecting on what she can do to ensure she makes more general eye contact. But this still isn't Action Research, because it is lacking that vital ingredient of 'seeing what works' or reflecting on the consequences of an intervention or change of strategy. In fact, we could argue that what Clare is doing isn't any kind of research at all. She's simply checking out for herself whether what her mentor has told her is true before she bothers doing anything about it. When she does reach the stage of doing something about it, that is when the opportunity will be there to undertake some Action Research.

- Ernest, in his role as team leader, presents us with a rather different scenario. The area of professional practice that he is working to develop is that of leadership skills. He's looking for the best way to support Bob, and the approach he is taking follows an Action Research model. This case reminds us that Action Research is not the sole preserve of teachers. It can be used to explore and develop a whole range of professional skills, and is particularly useful for transformational leadership, for management and for mentoring – all those areas of professionalism in FE and training which involve relationships but are not necessarily to do with those between teacher and learners. As Ernest tries one approach after another with Bob in an effort to find a leadership strategy which will provide the necessary support and reassurance, his interventions and reflections are following the classic Action Research spiral. Let's hope that he succeeded eventually in finding a strategy that enabled both Bob and himself to grow with confidence in their respective roles.

- And finally we had Zaneb who decides to try out various ways of introducing note-taking into her lessons in order to find the most effective way of developing those skills in her students. She is focusing on her own practice. She is experimenting to see what happens when she tries something new. Her purpose is to improve the quality of her students' learning experience and her own range of skills for supporting them. This fits neatly into the basic model of classroom-based Action Research.

So we've seen that what Bashir, Ernest and Zaneb are planning qualifies as Action Research. Annie and Frankie, on the other hand, are planning *practitioner research*, which is linear rather than cyclical and does not necessarily focus on their own practice. What Clare plans should probably be called self-observation. It's not cyclical and it's aimed at checking out something she's been told about herself rather than at finding new ways of improving practice.

CLOSE FOCUS CLOSE FOCUS CLOSE FOCUS CLOSE FOCUS CLOSE FOCUS

Let's pause for a moment here and think about Action Research in relation to the ethical guidelines for educational research which we discussed in Chapter 2. Read again through the list of projects above and decide which of them would require the researcher to obtain consent from the participants involved. When you've arrived at your own answer, check it out with the answer below.

Action Research and consent

Annie will need her learners' informed consent if she wants them to complete a learning styles questionnaire for the purposes of her own research. This is because she is asking them to reveal information about themselves.

Bashir, on the other hand, is not requiring information from his learners. He is observing his own failures and successes as he tries out various strategies. His learners aren't active 'participants' and there is therefore nothing for them to give their consent *to*.

Frankie will need to obtain informed consent from those colleagues whom he plans to observe. *Their* practice, not his own, is the central focus of his research.

Clare, even though her plan to have herself video recorded doesn't necessarily constitute 'research', will nevertheless need to obtain consent from the learners if they, too, are to be filmed. Of course, she may arrange to have the camera focused only on herself rather than on a wider view of the classroom. That's all she'd need, after all, to observe where she's directing her gaze. In that case, she wouldn't need learners' consent.

Ernest will focus on strategies for developing skills relating to his own role as team leader. He doesn't need Bob's consent to do this, because he, Ernest, is the focus of his own research.

Zaneb, too, in trying out various ways of introducing note-taking, is making herself the focus of her research. She doesn't need the consent of her learners to do this.

To summarise then: the simple model of Action Research which three of these characters propose using will not require anyone's consent, since it will be a reflective experiment or activity centred on the researcher themselves.

Action Research and the reflective journal

Because of the reflective nature of Action Research it is usual for the researcher to keep a journal during the planning and process of the research. This record of the researcher's reflections, ideas, critical incidents and progress over time can then be used as a source to be quoted when the research is written up. Because this model of research centres on the actions and professional and personal development of the researcher, a personal account such as a journal is ideally suited to the mapping of a such a journey and the personal reflections along the way. We can see an example of this in the extract below taken from Zaneb's research journal. As you read it through, look out for: a) reflection; b) critical incidents; c) action planning.

Zaneb's reflective journal

23 October

I suppose I shouldn't be surprised at the students' lack of note-taking skills. After all, it's not something that just comes naturally, and if they've never been taught how to do it, it's not their fault. It's made me realise that I must look carefully at my expectation of this group. The fact that they are adults could tempt me to assume a higher level of prior knowledge and skills than is actually the case. In fact, it has done – and not just about note-taking. Staying aware of my own assumptions and preconceptions is quite difficult. I have to stop every now and again and think, 'Is this a reasonable thing to suppose, or do I need to check it out before acting on it?' For example, I just assumed that George wouldn't mind feeding back on behalf of his group, because he always seems so confident and has so much to say (!), but it was clear I put him on the spot and he was really nervous.

So I still need to find a way to help them all learn to make notes without making them feel inadequate. The gapped handouts I tried yesterday didn't work too well. I think they were seen as a bit patronising. I must make sure that whatever I try will also reinforce their confidence rather than undermine it. Today, I tried the 'Reporter and Member of the Public' game. I gave a short presentation – a sort of mini-lecture – and then put them to work in pairs, the 'Reporter' interviewing the 'Member of the Public' about the content of the presentation. The idea was that between them they should come up with a headline and five sub-headings which would summarise the content. It worked quite well because a) they all produced good

> summaries of the main point; b) it was fun; and c) no one was exposed individually – it was a shared endeavour. But when I did the evaluation at the end of the lesson it was clear that quite a few of them were worried that we'd wasted time 'playing' when there's so much lesson content to get through in such a short time. So, it's back to the drawing board. But I have discovered some useful things. Working in pairs makes them feel more confident. They don't like any approach that seems to treat them like school-children. And they're all able to identify and summarise the main points of a presentation. So this is progress. Now I need to think about how to use what I've discovered to come up with a way of developing their note-taking skills that will succeed from every angle!

Notice particularly where Zaneb is reflecting on the purpose of her research; the possible reasons for progress or the lack of it; how she interprets what is happening; and how her own understanding is developing. Towards the end of this chapter we'll see how extracts from a reflective journal might be used to illustrate some of the points you make when you come to write up your research for others to read.

CLOSE FOCUS CLOSE FOCUS CLOSE FOCUS CLOSE FOCUS CLOSE FOCUS

Do you agree with Zaneb's interpretations of what is happening? Are there alternative ways of interpreting the data so far? Apart from the students' responses and reactions to her interventions, is there anything else Zaneb could be monitoring and reflecting on?

Other types of Action Research

Before that, however, we need to note that 'Action Research' is a broad category and includes processes, purposes and modes of inquiry other than the basic, rather instrumental model we've been looking at here so far, which, because it lends itself well to practical problem solving, proves so useful for teachers. Alternative models of Action Research include ones aimed at encouraging or facilitating social or political change (for example, Carr and Kemis, 1986). They also include those aimed at promoting and enabling social justice (for example, Griffiths, 2003). Some focus on collaborative practice, carried out by co-researchers; or on developing theory about best practice which can then be adopted or 'lived' to bring about transformations in relationships, institutions and ways of working (for example, the Living Theory Action Research of Whitehead and McNiff, 2006). Depending on the approach, they may include a critique of the assumptions and preconceptions underlying the choice or wording of the research question itself. But what all these types of Action Research have in common is a cyclical approach, a focus on change, and the prioritising of improvement in practice.

The existence of such a range of theories, emphases and approaches means that it's always important to explain clearly, when you're writing up your Action Research, exactly what you have taken the term to mean and why. To justify your approach you will need to cite recognised sources or previously published research which has interpreted the term in the same way. In the task below you'll see an example of how to do this.

TASK TASK TASK TASK TASK TASK TASK

Read the following extract from an Action Research project assignment. Bashir has been asked to hand this extract to his tutor for initial comment. In it, Bashir explains why he has chosen to use an Action

Research approach. You'll notice that he also gives reasons for his use of this particular *type* of Action Research. Other things to look out for are his use of references to support the points he makes, and how he deals with the potential weaknesses or criticisms of the Action Research methodology. As you read this part of his assignment, consider the following questions and – if you would find it helpful – make a note of how you would answer them. You can then compare your own responses to the discussion of these questions which comes later.

- **Is there any part of this extract where Bashir could have used a diagram or chart to present what he is saying more clearly?**

- **Can you see any instances where he could have cited a source or a reference for an argument or piece of terminology, but does not? Are there any other referencing errors or omissions?**

- **What about the structure and organisation of this section of Bashir's research paper? Is there any content here you would not have included under Method or Methodology, but would have presented in a different section, such as Findings or Conclusion?**

- **Notice how he quotes from his reflective journal. Could he have presented this differently? Does this quote enhance his account of his research? If so, how? If not, why not?**

- **Look at what he says about anonymising. How successful do you think this will be?**

Method

I decided to use an Action Research approach because this fitted my purpose which was to extend my professional understanding and skills, through reflection on my own practice (Atkins and Wallace, 2012). I used a simple reflective practitioner approach aimed at developing my own professional skills and understanding (Wellington, 2000). My research question can be broken down into three main aims. These were to:

1. discover a way to encourage the small group of self-excluding girls to engage more actively with their learning;
2. at the same time, encourage them to interact more with the rest of the class;
3. extend my own professional understanding and range of strategies relating to inclusion and classroom dynamics.

Using a simple Action Research cycle (Atkins and Wallace, 2012), I first observed the situation, then reflected on what I needed to change, then made an intervention, then observed the outcome and reflected on whether the intervention had effectively addressed or resolved the problem. It was necessary to repeat this cycle several times, trying different interventions, before I found a strategy which began to engage these learners with classroom activities and interactions, although the success was quite limited, as I shall discuss in the section on my findings. Thus, my research became a spiral of inquiry. The unsuccessful interventions I tried were:

1. devising an activity which required all the learners to work in pre-specified groups, and allocating each of the quiet girls to a different group in the hopes that, individually, they would interact with their peers;
2. setting a task which required group presentations. The quiet girls were asked to work as a group on preparing their presentation, but were told they would not be forced to stand up and present it to the class. They engaged in little or no discussion and produced no collaborative work;
3. groupwork, organised in such a way so that two other learners joined the quiet girl group.

The final and partially successful intervention was to sit and work with the group myself. These interventions and their consequences are summarised here to provide a clear account of my method. They are discussed in detail under Findings.

Methodology

As many researchers point out, Action Research is a very subjective method. Drawing as it does on the researcher's observations and reflections it is inevitably open to accusations of researcher bias. But, as McNiff points out, this is, in a way, irrelevant since the whole focus of this sort of inquiry is on the practitioner's own practice. It is therefore required to be subjective. There is no claim that the findings of Action Research of the kind I have used are transferable or generalisable to other practitioners or to other contexts. This is only about me and my exploration of my own practice. It is not Critical Action Research aimed at social change or social justice (Carr and Kemis, 1986). Neither is it Living Theory Action Research (McNiff et al., 1996).

'I want to carry out a fairly simple experiment which will require me to reflect carefully on my own practice and particularly on the strategies I use and the sensitivity I display in relation to shy or self-excluding learners. The learners I'd particularly like to find a way to support is a small group of non-participating girls in my Marketing class and I'm wondering whether gender will become an issue here.'
Reflective Journal, 12 November

Ethics

The focus of this research is my own practice. I am the only participant. I therefore did not need to secure informed consent from anyone. However, I did need to consider issues about confidentiality and anon-ymity (BERA, 2011) and ensure that it was not possible to identify any of the learners in my classes. For that reason, I have used a fictional name for my college ('Cowslip College') and for my subject ('Bookbinding') in writing up this research.

References

Atkins, L. and Wallace, S. (2012) *Qualitative Research in Education*. London: Sage.

BERA (2011) British Educational Research Association Guidelines for Ethical Research. www.bera.ac.uk (accessed 14.05.13).

Carr, W. and Kemmis, S. (1986) *Becoming Critical: Education, Knowledge and Action Research*. Lewes: The Falmer Press.

McNiff, J., Lomax, P. and Whitehead, J. (1996) *You and Your Action Research Project*. London: Routledge.

Wellington, J. (2000) *Educational Research*. London: Continuum.

Discussion

1. Bashir could have used a diagram or chart to summarise, or even replace, his description of the Action Research cycle. His verbal description alone is rather cumbersome: *'I first observed the situation, then reflected on what I needed to change, then made an intervention, then observed the outcome and reflected on whether the intervention had effectively addressed or resolved the problem.'* He could present a second diagram, too, to illustrate his point about the consecutive interventions representing 'a spiral of inquiry'. The use of diagrams, tables and charts when writing up your research can be very helpful in clarifying and summarising processes, comparisons and key points for the reader. It also helps you to keep things clear in your own mind, too.

2. There are at least two instances where Bashir could (and should) have cited a source or a reference but does not. One is his rather general statement: *'As many researchers point out'*, for which he offers no evidence or examples. General or vague claims such as this should be avoided when writing up research unless you can follow them with a list of at least three examples in brackets. One, or even two examples won't do, because he's used the word 'many'. A second is where he uses the phrase 'a cycle of inquiry'. This term looks like something he has found in the course of his reading, and he should acknowledge the source. As well as these examples, did you notice that he cites McNiff in the third line of his methodology, but gives no date. Neither does he list a single authored work by McNiff in his references. This is going to be very frustrating for the reader because McNiff has written a great deal about Action Research (check online and you'll see), and so it's impossible to tell which work Bashir is referring to here. Does she really say this anywhere? How can we verify what he says if he fails to

reference it properly? He may even mean McNiff et al. (1996), which he does list in his references; but, if so, he has cited it here incorrectly.

3. What about the structure and organisation of this section of Bashir's research paper? If you take the view that his list of unsuccessful interventions and his summary of the intervention that came closest to succeeding would more sensibly belong in his Findings section, you may well have a point. It is very important to avoid unnecessary repetition when writing up research, as this can make your arguments appear muddled and unclear. Deciding where and how to sequence your content is not always easy; but a good rule to bear in mind is: if you're going to have to come back to this and say it again, don't say it now; save it for later, and explain to the reader that's what you're going to do. For example: *'The complications that arose at this point will be discussed in the next section, under "Findings".'*

4. What about the way he presents the quote from his reflective journal? Does it add anything to his account of his research? Well it does look rather as though he's just bolted it on as an afterthought, doesn't it? But it does add something to our understanding of his aims and starting point. For example, he mentions a concern with 'sensitivity', which is an element that hasn't come through anywhere else in this extract; and he reflects on whether gender might be 'an issue' – which is something we might have expected him to elaborate on somewhere in this method and methodology section. So it's an interesting journal entry. The problem is that he simply puts it there on the page with no introduction, and with no following comment. The result is that we are left to wonder why it's there, and how it relates to this section as a whole. Journal extracts, like any other quote, need weaving into your argument and into your text to become a logical part of the entirety. If you don't do that, they'll look bolt-on like this one, and will fail to serve your intended purpose.

5. And lastly, how successfully has Bashir maintained the anonymity of his learners? He's come up with a creative fictional name for the college, and has disguised the course he teaches on as 'bookbinding.' So far, so good. But he has neglected to edit the journal extract he uses, and so has accidentally identified the subject for all to see: Marketing. This information could potentially allow his learners to be identified – putting Bashir in breach of research ethics.

A SUMMARY OF **KEY POINTS**

In this chapter we have discussed:
> **what is meant by Action Research;**
> **the distinction between Action Research and linear practitioner research;**
> **questions we can ask ourselves to identify whether an inquiry conforms to an Action Research model;**
> **questions about Action Research and consent;**
> **the role of the reflective journal in Action Research;**
> **the range of models and approaches covered by the term 'Action Research'.**

We have also identified some useful terms to use when writing about Action Research. These include: *action research cycle; action research spiral; intervention; reflective practice; reflective journal; living theory; critical theory action research; cycles of action; practitioner research; cyclical.*

Branching options

You may like to choose one of the following activities which are designed to help you apply what you've learnt from this chapter to your own practice. The first encourages you, as a professional, to develop your skills of reflection; the second asks you to take an evaluative approach consistent with an initial teaching qualification in the sector; and the third is designed to support skills of critical analysis appropriate to post-qualification CPD or Masters level study.

Reflection

Read again the extract from Zaneb's reflective journal. How could the process she records here be represented in diagrammatic form?

Evaluation

Richard wants to carry out some Action Research as part of his professional development. The topic he is interested in is:

What can be done to prevent learners with excellent IT skills from disengaging in lessons while he is helping the less skilled?

How would you advise him to: a) word his title/research question; and b) design his process, so that it conforms to an Action Research model?

Critical analysis

Look again at how Bashir, in the extract from his assignment, has broken down his research question down into three research aims, all of which are consistent with his method of Action Research. Now do the same for: a) Zaneb's; and b) Ernest's research questions.

REFERENCES AND FURTHER READING

The following two books will help you to discover more about Action Research, and illustrate some of the range of Action Research theory or schools of thought. Carr and Kemmis (1986) is considered a classic text in Action Research. It argues persuasively that researching one's own field of practice is an essential characteristic of the professional; and presents a view of Action Research as *praxis* (reflection which leads to *action*, rather than simply to the acquisition of knowledge or insight). If you haven't time to read it all, you may find the first chapter, on teachers as researchers, most useful. McNiff et al. (1996) is in some ways an easier read. Aimed at the practitioner, it is helpful and straightforward. The authors are these days closely associated with Living Theory Action Research. McNiff's and Whitehead's work has diverged, seeming to argue that they now espouse slightly different theoretical positions in relation to Living Theory. This is a useful reminder that 'Action Research' is a term which encompasses a range of methodological approaches.

Carr, W. and Kemmis, S. (1986) *Becoming Critical: Education, Knowledge and Action Research*. Lewes: The Falmer Press.

McNiff, J., Lomax, P. and Whitehead, J. (1996) *You and Your Action Research Project*. London: Routledge.

You may also find the following two books useful. The first provides a more general introduction to Action Research in an educational context. The second has a useful and accessible first chapter on keeping a reflective journal, with clear guidance on what constitutes reflection and what does not.

Somek, B. and Noffke, S. (2008) *Handbook of Educational Action Research*. London: Sage.
Wallace, S. (2011) *Teaching, Tutoring and Training in the Lifelong Learning Sector* (4th edition). Exeter: Learning Matters.

Two further books cited in this chapter are:

Griffiths, M. (2003) *Action for Social Justice in Education: Fairly Different*. London: Open University Press.
Whitehead, J. and McNiff, J. (2006) *Action Research: Living Theory*. London: Sage.

5
Getting on the case:
case studies and insider research

The objectives of this chapter

This chapter introduces you to the advantages and potential pitfalls of using case study as a basis for your research. Most teachers and trainee-teachers who carry out research find it most useful to base their project in the college where they are doing their teaching. Their case studies, therefore, are often carried out as insider research, and so we shall also be exploring the advantages and disadvantages of conducting research inside your own institution. In the process, the chapter will revisit some key terminology, and introduce some which may be new or unfamiliar, including: *subjectivity; objectivity; reliability; validity; trustworthiness; situating the researcher; epistemology; grounded theory; unit of analysis; convergence of evidence;* as well as *case study* and *insider research*.

Introduction

Case studies are widely used in educational research. One reason for this is that they provide a way of exploring a question within its real-life setting. Another is that they are ideally suited to the small scale, classroom-based research which teachers find most useful when seeking to develop their own professional practice. Yin (2003: 13) describes case studies as a way to *investigate a contemporary phenomenon within its real-life context.* Here, 'contemporary' means 'happening now'. If we substitute for this the words *'professionally relevant'* we have a useful expression of why this method of research can suit our purposes so well as teachers and managers in FE and training. Let's take Dylan, for example, who suspects that the style of teaching he is adopting is at least partly driven by the need to keep unruly learners on task. He wonders whether this may be true of his colleagues, too. So, he decides to conduct some research, using his own department – Construction and Built Environment – as a *case study*. This will allow him to investigate this professionally relevant issue 'within its real-life context', as we have seen Yin suggest. We'll look at his story in a moment. But let's just note here that the researcher in this case – Dylan – will be collecting his data from inside his own institution. It will be *insider research*. This will present him with a whole set of advantages and disadvantages which are quite different to those that would arise if he were carrying out the research in a different college and was therefore approaching it as an outsider; and we'll be considering some of those advantages and disadvantages later in the chapter. Dylan will be using a case study approach to carry out insider research; but it is important to note here that, although we are looking at the two together, case studies do not necessarily have to be carried out by insiders, as we shall see.

TASK TASK TASK TASK TASK **TASK** TASK TASK TASK **TASK** TASK

Read the following account of Dylan's research and consider the following questions:
• **How do Dylan's methods of data collection complement each other?**

- Dylan has chosen to base his research on practice within his department. How might it have changed the nature and significance of his question if he had: a) chosen to research only his own teaching; or b) collected data from across the whole college?

- Why would it have been useful to have elicited additional data, such as the respondent's age, length of experience, and specific subject taught?

- His interviewees are volunteers. Could this present any problems in relation to the data?

- How would you summarise the stages of Dylan's research, using bullet points?

- In what ways is Dylan's status as an insider of advantage to him in this research?

- In what ways could it be seen as a disadvantage?

- Does Dylan comply with the BERA ethical guidelines throughout his research?

- You may find it useful to make a note of your answers as you go along, so that you can compare them with the answers given in the discussion which follows this section.

Dylan's insider case study

Dylan realises that he will need his colleagues' co-operation and agreement if he is to carry out his research successfully. The first question he has to address is what data he will need in order to answer his questions. In some ways, it is quite a delicate question and he has to phrase it in a way that doesn't imply any criticism of colleagues' practice nor of learner behaviour. The first version he comes up with is: *'When planning your lessons, to what extent do you take into account the risk of disruptive learner behaviour?'* But after careful consideration he decides that this is no good for two reasons. One problem is that word 'extent'. It's too vague. What one teacher calls 'a great extent' another might define as 'to some extent', and so on. This means he wouldn't be able to present his findings and conclusions in any meaningful way. After thinking this through for some time, Dylan decides to limit his case study to a 'snapshot' of one week, and to ask his colleagues, *'When designing your lesson plans for last week, have any of your planning decisions been informed by the need to avoid or counter the possibility of unco-operative or disruptive learner behaviour?'* He will follow this by two more questions: 1. 'If you have answered "yes", how many of your lesson plans last week does this apply to?' and 2. 'How many lessons did you plan over all last week?' These are designed to give him some indication of the extent to which this is a real issue.

He distributes a questionnaire with these three questions on it to all 24 colleagues in the department, including part-time colleagues and two trainee-teachers. Only after he has given them out and received 18 back completed does he realise it would have been useful to have elicited additional data, such as the respondent's age, length of experience, and specific subject taught. He follows up the questionnaires by interviewing five colleagues who have the ticked the box indicating that they would be willing to do this. He asks them more detailed questions about their lesson planning. They all seem to share an interest in how to motivate learners and encourage positive behaviour. One of them points out that teachers may often change or adapt their lesson plan in mid-lesson in response to behaviour issues or learners' obvious disengagement, and that Dylan's research methods as they stand won't show this up. So Dylan seeks permission from colleagues to observe some taught sessions. Three colleagues agree to invite him in and to provide him with a copy of their lesson plan so that he can observe whether negative learner behaviour at any point triggers deviation from the plan. He also has the opportunity to observe one of the trainee-teachers because he is her mentor. He decides he doesn't need to seek her permission in relation to the research because he would be observing her anyway.

When he comes to write up his case study he is able to conclude that the management of student behaviour does appear to be a factor in teachers' lesson planning within his department, with 11 out of 18 respondents answering in the affirmative. From the interviews he is able to report that participants consider 'behaviour' to be a learner characteristic which, like other characteristics such as numeracy or literacy levels, age and previous qualifications, must be taken into account when planning. And from the four classes observed he concludes that teachers who stick rigidly to their lesson plan (in this case, the trainee-teacher) do not effectively address learners' negative or non-compliant behaviour.

Discussion

In the end, Dylan uses three methods of data collection in his case study: questionnaires, interviews and observations.

1. So, how do Dylan's methods of data collection complement each other? Well, he has chosen to collect both quantitative and qualitative data. The questionnaire will provide him with teachers' account of *how many* of their lessons are planned with behaviour management in mind, and *what proportion* this constitutes of their lessons over all. The interviews allow him to ask more complex questions and discover colleagues' *views and opinions* about the significance of this issue. The classroom observations are an opportunity to *see for himself* what is happening, rather than rely only on others' accounts of their own practice and of the values which inform it. Seeing for himself, however, does not mean that the data thus gathered are somehow more objective or 'true' than what he has been told in the questionnaires and interviews, because, like any observer, he is likely to see what he is looking for, but may well miss significant data he hasn't thought to seek. But having information from these three separate sources does mean that he is able to employ *methodological triangulation*. If this triangulation shows a *convergence of evidence* – that is, if data collected via the various methods all seems to point to the same conclusion – he can take it as an indication of the reliability of his data over all. And because he has used a combination of quantitative and qualitative data gathering we can say that he has employed a *mixed methods* approach, rather than simply relying on one research instrument (such as a questionnaire) and the one set of data it produces. As we've already seen, a mixed methods approach is useful in supporting claims about the reliability of your research outcomes.

2. Our next question was: How might it change the nature and significance of Dylan's question if he had a) chosen to research only his own teaching; or b) collected data from across the whole college? If he had chosen to focus only on his own professional practice, Dylan would have been carrying out simple linear practitioner research. If he had focused on his own practice *with the intention of exploring how he could bring about change*, he would be using an Action Research model. On the other hand, if he had based his research on data from across the whole college, he would still have been taking a case study approach, but we would say that his *unit of analysis* was the college rather than just one department or vocational area within that college. Your choice of unit of analysis for case study research will determine the scope you have for employing a range of data collection methods – the larger the unit, the wider the possibilities; and it will also have implications for the questions you might consider about *transferability or generalisability* of your findings. For example, Dylan's research might be telling us something useful about one department or one vocational area in one college, and we might want to investigate further to discover whether the same findings would be obtained in the same vocational area in different college, or in different vocational areas in the same college. If his unit of analysis had been provision across the entire college, we would be asking different questions, such as: would the findings be the same at a different college? Is this an FE phenomenon? Is such planning around behaviour a characteristic of FE provision everywhere? On the other

hand, if his unit of analysis had simply been his own practice, any questions about transferability would have to begin with: Is this just me? Does anyone else do this?

3. Dylan regrets, in retrospect, not asking for *demographic information* about the questionnaire respondents, such as their age or length of professional experience. Why? Well, this additional data would allow him to provide a more complex analysis of his findings. For example, he might have identified a *correlation* between length of experience and an approach to lesson planning which built in alternative activities to meet all contingencies; or between early career teachers and flexibility of lesson planning. Demographic details add to the *richness and complexity* of data which is one of the characteristic strengths of case study research. The emphasis that Yin (2009) places on the *real-life* context of case studies should always be born in mind. Real life itself is complex and rich in detail, and it is part of the purpose of case studies to capture this. What is more, the absence of demographic detail can lead to difficulties and misunderstandings when it comes to interpreting findings. For example, one of the four teachers whom Dylan observes is the trainee-teacher he mentors. We are told that she sticks rigidly to her lesson plan. Well, she would, wouldn't she? There she is, being observed by her mentor, knowing that she'll be graded on lesson planning. It's not likely that she'll deviate from that plan under any circumstances other than a full-scale riot. But none of this context will show up in Dylan's findings. Presented bluntly on the page it will appear as: *'One in four of the teachers observed stuck rigidly to their lesson plan and thereby did not effectively address learners' negative or non-compliant behaviour.'* This is misleading for the reader because they have here only half the story.

4. The colleagues whom Dylan interviews are all volunteers. This is one way to 'select' participants, and we'll be considering other ways in the chapters which follow. Certainly, using volunteers as participants has the advantage that the interviewees will be interested and co-operative and not likely to resent the demand on their time. But there's also a disadvantage, which is that they will not constitute a 'typical' sample group. The very fact that they have volunteered probably means that they are interested in the topic or in research, or both; and are willing to give you their time. Why does this matter? Because the people who have not volunteered demonstrably do not share these characteristics. Dylan's interviewees, therefore, are not simply a random group of teachers from the department; they are a specific group with specific interests or attitudes. The findings from the interviews are unlikely to be the same as if Dylan had picked out interviewees with a pin, at random. This has implications for the reliability and trustworthiness of his research.

5. Yin (2009:1) identifies six distinct stages in case study research. They are:
   - **planning;**
   - **designing;**
   - **preparing;**
   - **collecting;**
   - **analysing;**
   - **sharing.**

So, let's see how Dylan's inquiry fits into this pattern.

Stage	Activity
Planning	Dylan suspects that the style of teaching he is adopting is at least partly driven by the need to keep unruly learners on task. He wonders whether this may be true of his colleagues, too. So he decides to conduct some research, using his own department – Construction and Built Environment – as a *case study*.
Designing	The first question he has to address is what data he will need in order to answer his questions. He arrives at a research question after some reflection and re-drafting. His initial research design involves a questionnaire to all departmental colleagues, followed by interviews with five volunteers.
Preparing	He prepares the questionnaires and the interview questions. *At this preparation stage he should also be: (i) reading research texts to find out about questionnaire and interview design; and (ii) exploring the literature relating to lesson planning and behaviour.*
Collecting	He distributes questionnaires and 18 out of 24 are completed and returned. *He realises at this stage that it would have been useful to include questions to establish the demographic.* He conducts interviews and realises from an interviewee's comments that *he really needs to include some lesson observations.*
Analysing	He analyses his data and comes to the conclusion that the management of student behaviour does appear to be a factor in teachers' lesson planning within his department. *He also draws conclusions based on his observation of the trainee-teacher which do not take the power relationship between researcher and this particular participant into account.*
Sharing	He writes up his research, but we don't know yet how he will disseminate it.

Italics have been used in the table to show where Dylan has run into difficulties, been insufficiently prepared, or failed to think sufficiently clearly about the implications of his decisions. We can see from this that the planning and designing stages are crucial. Dylan gets into difficulties because he has not given sufficient thought to these early stages. It is a common mistake for teachers new to research to want to jump in there as soon as possible and start collecting data. Dylan's experience shows us that this can lead to all sorts of trouble, from missed opportunities for data to misinterpretation of evidence and erroneous conclusions.

6. Our next question was about Dylan's status as an insider. This was probably an advantage for him in that he was able to secure the co-operation of colleagues. They might have been more willing to spare the time to complete his questionnaire since they know him. He has also been able to observe classes quite easily without having to seek institutional permission, seek clearance, write letters of request and so on.

7. However, there are disadvantages to being an insider. You may have thought of some of the following:

- It will be more difficult for him to be objective, because his familiarity with the college means that he will come to the research with preconceived ideas about people and systems.
- Insider research may raise problems with anonymity and confidentiality. For example, when he writes up his paper under his own name it will be easy for anyone to identify his college, even if he fictionalises its name and location.
- The potential for easy access to people, data, classes and so on will present him with additional ethical dilemmas; and there may be a temptation to overstep the mark and ignore ethical guidelines by, for example, using every day access to covertly gather data.

8. We see an example of this last point when Dylan decides he doesn't need to seek the trainee-teacher's permission in relation to the research because, as her mentor, he would be observing her anyway. *This is completely unacceptable*. He is treating her simply as a source of data, and ignoring the guidelines on ethics that require the researcher to ensure that all participants have given their informed consent to be part of the inquiry.

CLOSE FOCUS CLOSE FOCUS CLOSE FOCUS CLOSE FOCUS CLOSE FOCUS

Dylan has used questionnaires, interviews and observations. Think back to discussions in previous chapters about the trustworthiness and reliability of data. Which of Dylan's methods within this case study do you think will yield the most reliable data, and why?

Reliability, validity, epistemology

Let's look more closely now at some of the issues raised in Discussion point 1. We've encountered these sorts of questions before, for example in Chapter 3 during the discussion between Di, Raj, Hamish and their tutor. At one point Di and Raj seemed to suggest that the views or opinions which people might express in reply to Hamish's research question (*'Why do so many people think it's smarter to study A levels in a sixth form than a level 3 qualification in FE?'*) can't be taken as valuable or trustworthy data for the purposes of research. And yet they don't have these reservations about Hamish's revised question, which has now become: *'What do level 3 learners in FE consider to be the advantages and disadvantages of studying for a vocational qualification in an FE college rather than studying A levels in school?'* You were asked to think about a) why this seemed less problematical to them; and b) how we might reword Hamish's original question so that the data it generated could be considered more reliable. You might like to look again at the notes you made in response to this task, because we're going to discuss the answer to that question now in terms of validity, reliability and epistemology.

Validity

To be considered *valid*, data must be gathered in an appropriate form from an appropriate source, as we saw briefly in Chapter 1. For example, if you wanted to discover what students' career aspirations are, you would ask the students themselves. This would produce data that was valid. But if you asked their teachers or their parents; or if you tried to extrapolate this information from their attainment scores; or if you tried to deduce an answer from examining their completed learning styles questionnaires, the data you would gather would be of limited validity. This was one of the problems with Hamish's original research question. He wanted to ask 'people' why other 'people' held a particular view. The data this question would have produced would have limited validity, because it would only be speculation.

Reliability

When we say that data is *reliable* we mean that the same data would have emerged if a different researcher had asked the same questions, or if the same researcher had asked those questions at a different time. In other words, the findings have not been determined by the identity of the researcher, their relative power in relation to the participants, or their bias or preconceptions in the phrasing or presentation of the research question/s. For example, a teacher asking her learners questions about their college experience might receive unreliable responses simply because the power relationship leads them to provide answers that they think the teacher wants. Hamish's original question pre-supposes that 'so many people' hold certain attitudes, thereby building his own pre-conceptions into the question from the start.

Epistemology

Epistemology is derived from a Greek word meaning *'theory of knowledge'*. We all have our own theories about what constitutes knowledge, or what some people would call 'truth'. For example, I'm comfortable about taking what participants tell me about themselves as a basis for making the claim that I know something about them. I'm happy to take qualitative data – what I hear or read people saying or what I see them doing – as evidence from which to draw conclusions or construct new knowledge. Not all researchers feel as I do, however. Some take the epistemological position that such qualitative data is not a sufficiently sound basis on which to make claims about *knowing.* If you have a background in the sciences, for example, it is possible that you may be more comfortable with data which doesn't rely on what people say, but which instead is measurable and observable. This would mean that your epistemological position is different to mine, which is to say that you have a different set of criteria for determining whether you 'know' something. This is a challenging debate that we shall find ourselves returning to several times in the chapters which follow.

Hamish's questions

So if we go back to Hamish's questions we can see now that there's an epistemological problem here because his first version is basically asking for people's opinion about why other people hold certain opinions! It is also making an assumption about what people think, rather than seeking evidence that they do. (*'Why do so many people think it's smarter to study A levels in a sixth form than a level 3 qualification in FE?'*) This means that the data would be doubly untrustworthy. It would consist of guesswork by some people about other people's views. And if we ask ourselves the basic epistemological question: *Can we accept the data this question generates as a basis on which to claim that we now 'know' something?* – the answer is clearly no. And yet the question or title is phrased in such a way as to suggest that the research will be able to come up with a definitive answer.

Hamish's second question, however, doesn't meet with such objections from his colleagues. (*'What do level 3 learners in FE consider to be the advantages and disadvantages of studying for a vocational qualification in an FE college rather than studying A levels in school?'*) This is because he has changed tack here and is asking *what* people think, rather than *why*, so his question is much more straightforward. To find out learners' views he will be asking the learners themselves, which means that his data is more likely to be valid. He'll be seeking their views first hand, which means his data will have a greater level of reliability. As a consequence, the data he collects will be a more trustworthy basis for Hamish to claim that he has generated knowledge through his research, and he will be better able to justify his epistemological position.

TASK TASK **TASK** TASK **TASK** **TASK** TASK **TASK** TASK **TASK** **TASK** TASK

We've seen Dylan engaging in insider research with his college-based case study. Let's see what happens now when he extends his research and looks for answers to the same questions in two local school sixth forms. Here he will be conducting case study research as an *outsider* in an unfamiliar environment, both in terms of place and sector. His mentor suggests that Dylan begins to write up this new phase of his research as part of a professional development journal. You'll see a section of this below. Read it through carefully and note down any points you think the mentor might want to discuss with Dylan. We'll pick up what some of these might be after the journal extract.

April 24th

When I made the decision to extend the research into local sixth forms I also decided to keep to the case study approach and use the same methods of data collection, as this would make the comparison of data between the two case studies more reliable than if I started using a completely different set of methods. I'm taking the two sixth forms together as my unit of inquiry, although obviously I'm visiting them separately to carry out the research. But having collected data from one of the case study schools I've noticed a big difference between researching in my own institution and coming in as an outside researcher into the participants' environment. Leaving aside the practical difficulties over access arrangements, there was a notable difference in the return rate of questionnaires. Out of 30 distributed to teachers, only 12 were returned completed. None of these had the box ticked indicating the participant was willing to be interviewed. When I asked around, person to person, there seemed to be some suspicion about my purpose. Some mistrust was expressed, and it became clear that some teachers thought the college was out to 'poach' students away from the sixth form. When I took my concerns to the head teacher, she seemed to think that my questions about planning and non-compliant behaviour were somehow a reflection on the levels of discipline in her school. Eventually, I persuaded two teachers to be interviewed. Their responses were very brief and they refused to be drawn into elaborating on any of their answers. The same two also gave informed consent (reluctantly, I think) for me to observe them teaching. I felt awkward because I was clearly unwelcome, and this made it difficult for me to get very much out of the observations. Also, I got the impression that they were 'performing' for me and that what I saw were not typical sixth form lessons.

But I have all my data now, from college and from school. So now I'm going to begin my reading of journal papers about the impact of learner behaviour on lesson planning. Doing it this way around – collecting and interrogating data first, and then using what you find there to guide your choice of reading – is known as Grounded Theory. This works well for me, because I wasn't sure what my data was going to tell me. I wanted to ask a genuine question and look for a genuine answer. I didn't want to go into the research with preconceived ideas about what I'd find, otherwise that could have meant I'd be asking leading questions, which would affect the reliability of my data.

Discussion

I'm not so sure that Dylan doesn't ask leading questions; but we'll let that go for now. Some of the points that his mentor may want to pick up on include the following:

- ***The problems facing him as an outside researcher.*** Practical problems about access are obviously a nuisance; but the problems that should most concern a researcher are those which may affect the reliability or validity of the data. The low return rate for questionnaires is potentially a problem because the fewer responses, the less likely it is that they represent the staff over all and the less confident Dylan can be that the data from them can be treated as a reliable indication of planning practices across the sixth form. The unwillingness of staff to be interviewed presents the same problem. Can Dylan take the responses of only two reluctant interviewees as a reliable snapshot of staff practices as a whole? Not really. And the observations he carries out obviously do not convince him that he's seeing 'the real thing'. So there's a question mark over the reliability of this part of his data, too.

- *Persuading two teachers to be interviewed.* Persuasion doesn't sit very comfortably with informed consent. It also seems to result in the interviewees refusing to be drawn into elaborating on any of their answers. A question that Dylan's mentor might want to raise here is: *What was gained by conducting these interviews?* If interviewees are unwilling to elaborate and provide only very brief answers, the data might as well be gathered by questionnaire. One of the great advantages of the interview, as we'll see in a later chapter, is the flexibility it provides to pursue lines of questioning and dig deeper for answers. Dylan hasn't been able to do this here. We must also ask: *How might reluctance to be interviewed affect the reliability of the responses?*

- *Observation or performance?* Dylan was given the impression that the two teachers he observed were 'performing'. This must make him question the reliability of any data gained from these observations, since his own presence seems to have created an artificial context. If these two teachers had carried out peer observations of one another, they might have seen something quite different.

- *The outsider.* As an outside researcher, Dylan has the advantage of a greater degree of objectivity, and he avoids problems that might arise from unequal power relationships between himself and participants in his own college. But he encounters some real disadvantages, too, including levels of suspicion and reluctance to participate which could affect the reliability of any data he gathers. He will also be unaware of issues and relationships which may lie beneath the surface; and will have a limited understanding of the experience of teaching in a school. In his own college environment he has a complex understanding of key issues and current concerns which will help him to make better sense of his data. He doesn't mention this in his journal entry. Perhaps it's a distinction between insider and outsider research which he has yet to reflect upon.

CLOSE FOCUS CLOSE FOCUS CLOSE FOCUS CLOSE FOCUS

Grounded theory

Dylan mentions grounded theory, which is an approach often used in qualitative research, and was developed by Glaser and Strauss in the 1960s. A more recent edition of their work is *The Discovery of Grounded Theory* (1999). As is the case with Action Research, there are several interpretations of grounded theory, and even Glaser and Strauss themselves came eventually to disagree about what it was and what it was not. However, there is general agreement that, instead of taking a theory or hypothesis as a starting point for research, the grounded theory approach is to begin with data collection and then proceed to develop a theory based upon that data. The data is used to determine what literature is relevant to the inquiry, rather than the literature being used to influence the research design, as it would be, for example, if you were testing a theory or hypothesis. In other words, the theory is *grounded* in 'what is' as represented by the data. Therefore, a review of the literature and reflection on theory follows the data collection rather than preceding it. Because he has begun his data collection before exploring the literature, Dylan claims that he is using a grounded theory approach, but there is an aspect of his research which tells us that he has not really understood how grounded theory works in practice. Can you see what it is? For the answer, look back at the earlier section where he formulates his research question.

A SUMMARY OF **KEY POINTS**

In this chapter we have discussed:
> the advantages of using a case study approach in research, including the opportunities it provides for methodological triangulation and the use of mixed methods;
> the advantages and pitfalls of insider research;
> the relationship between units of analysis and the transferability or generalisability of research findings;
> the importance of demographic detail in providing the richness and complexity of data that case studies allow;
> the crucial importance of the planning and design stages of case study research;
> the meaning of *reliability* and *validity* in a case study context;
> how grounded theory differs from a traditional research approach.

We have also identified some useful terms to use when writing about case studies and insider research. These include: *subjectivity; objectivity; reliability; validity; trustworthiness; situating the researcher; epistemology; grounded theory; unit of analysis; convergence of evidence.*

Branching options

You may like to choose one of the following activities which are designed to help you apply what you've learnt from this chapter to your own practice. The first encourages you, as a professional, to develop your skills of reflection; the second asks you to take an evaluative approach consistent with an initial teaching qualification in the sector; and the third is designed to support skills of critical analysis appropriate to post-qualification CPD or Masters level study.

Reflection

What could Dylan have done differently at the planning and design stages to ensure that his reception in the case study sixth form was a more positive one?

Evaluation

We've discussed how useful case study research can be to the FE practitioner. But it is not without its dangers. The following are common pitfalls. Does Dylan avoid them, and if so, how?

1. The temptation to make generalised claims from one case study. For example, *'This suggests that all teachers...'* or *'all colleges'* or *'all of FE...'*
2. Neglecting to obtain informed consent from all or any participants.
3. Lack of rigour. For example, researcher bias.

Critical analysis

Evaluate each of Dylan's methods for data collection in terms of their validity and reliability. Which do you consider: a) most reliable; and b) most valid, and why?

What could he have done differently at the planning and design stage that would have improved the levels of reliability and validity of his data?

REFERENCES AND FURTHER READING REFERENCES AND FURTHER READING

The following two books provide more detailed discussion of case study research and insider research respectively.

Costley, C., Elliot, G. and Gibbs, P. (2010) *Doing Work-based Research: Approaches to Inquiry for Insider Researchers.* London: Sage.

Yin, R. (2009) *Case Study Research: Design and Methods* (4th edition). London: Sage.

If you would like to read more about grounded theory, you may find the following useful:

Glaser, B.J. and Strauss, A.L. (1999) *The Discovery of Grounded Theory*. Chicago, IL: Aldine Transactions.

Strauss, A.L. and Corbin, J. (1997) *Grounded Theory in Practice*. London: Sage.

6
Questions and answers: questionnaires and focus groups

The objectives of this chapter

This chapter explores the use of surveys and questionnaires, looking at topics such as questionnaire design and choice of participants. It also discusses the use of focus groups, since these are a useful way of involving students as participants while maintaining their anonymity and avoiding asking for individual responses from students in age groups which may be deemed 'vulnerable' (for example, 14–16-year-olds). The chapter will revisit some key research terminology, such as: *data triangulation; respondent; analysis of data; correlation; anonymity;* and introduce some which may be new or unfamiliar, such as: *open and closed questions; Likert scale; focus group.*

Introduction

A questionnaire survey is often the first thing that springs to mind when someone mentions research. Compared to interviews and observations, for example, they are certainly a very useful way of collecting data from the maximum number of participants in the minimum time. The same is also true of focus groups. And, of course, both these methods have the additional advantage that they make it relatively easy for the researcher to maintain the anonymity of participants. But that is not to say that either of them is somehow an easy option. They are not. Both these methods require the researcher to carry out careful planning, preparation and reflection, preferably including a pilot or trial run, before the research is conducted. Failure to do so can lead to useless, missing or unreliable data; or to data which reflects a researcher bias. So first of all we're going to follow two researchers through their questionnaire design and discover some rules for success. Then we're going to turn our attention to using focus groups as a research method and consider what advantages, if any, it might have over the use of questionnaires.

Ashraf designs a questionnaire

Ashraf teaches Performing Arts at a large city FE college. He finds his learners, on the whole, to be lacking in motivation and reluctant to engage in individual performance. He's started to wonder what made them choose this vocational area, given that they seem to show so little enthusiasm for it. He has to undertake a piece of small-scale research as part of his professional development, so he decides to take these concerns as his research focus. He has a long commute to work, a full teaching timetable and now this assignment to complete for his professional qualification. Feeling pressed for time, he thinks that probably a questionnaire would be the quickest way to get this research done; and so he spends an hour or so designing one.

TASK TASK TASK TASK TASK TASK TASK TASK TASK TASK TASK

You can see the questionnaire that Ashraf produced below. In order to evaluate a questionnaire it is sometimes helpful to think about how you would respond to each question yourself. So look through it carefully and make a note of anything you think Ashraf should consider changing, and why.

Questionnaire

Thank you for completing this questionnaire. The data will be used as part of my professional research project. You are not required to identify yourself. All responses will be treated confidentially.

1. Why did you choose to study Performing Arts?
   a) I want to be an actor
   b) I want to be a singer
   c) I want to be a director/make-up artist/lighting technician

2. Did you study Performing Arts at school?
   a) Yes
   b) No

3. Why?

4. What do you enjoy about Performing Arts?
   a) Performing
   b) Backstage roles
   c) Theory

5. How do you think you will be able to work in the PA world if you don't like performing?

6. How old are you?

7. Sex?

8. Who made the decision for you to enrol on the Performing Arts course?
   a) You
   b) Your parents

9. Do you regret being on the Performing Arts course?

10. What would you rather be doing?
    a) Another course at college
    b) Staying on at school

Discussion

Here is some feedback from Ashraf's tutor. See how many of the points she raises are ones you have already identified.

Tutor feedback form

Ashraf, I've read through your draft questionnaire and I can see that you've used a combination of open and closed questions, which is always a good idea because it allows for the possibility that you may discover something in the open answers that you hadn't previously thought of. It also means that the questionnaires will yield both qualitative and quantitative data which will allow you to look for connections and correlations between the two.

But there are also quite a lot of problems with this questionnaire, and so I'm going to give you what I hope are helpful comments question by question before giving more general feedback and advice.

- First, your rubric at the top. You say that all responses will be treated confidentially, but that's not quite the case. You're going to be using these responses as data in a research assignment. What you mean here is that all responses will be treated anonymously. Confidentiality is not the same thing as anonymity.
- Q1 includes no instructions. You need something such as: 'circle your chosen answer' or 'tick your chosen answer'. If you don't do this you can't be sure, for example, whether a respondent who puts a cross against an option is indicating a positive rather than a negative choice. Also, you've got disparate career choices lumped together here, which will make the responses difficult to analyse. A director's role is a very different from a lighting engineer's. Putting them together like this will make your findings unclear. And thirdly, you haven't provided an 'other' category. See also my comments on question 10.
- Q2 and 3: Why would this information be useful to you? And if you're going to ask a question about previous study, wouldn't it better to ask 'what' rather than 'why'? For example, what level did they study PA at? Did it involve performance? How did they feel about that? And so on. Also you need to think about the space you allow for open questions. There's so little allowed here that it would be difficult for the learner to fit in more than three or four words.
- Q4: You've limited their choice of responses here. What if it was none of those, but something else which you've not thought of but which might be crucial to your understanding of why there's a lack of motivation? This is an example of the researcher's preconceived ideas imposing limits on the data it'll be possible to gather. In other words, you're causing some potential answers to disappear before you start. And what about asking them what they don't enjoy? Wouldn't this be a better way to get at reasons why they don't appear motivated?
- Q5: This looks more like an accusation than a question! First of all you're putting words in their mouth. Not all your students dislike performing, surely? Secondly, this presents as a *rhetorical* question – that is, one which makes a point rather than genuinely seeks an answer. What sort of answers would you expect to get here? And whatever they might be, there's again very little space to put them in!
- Q6: From what I remember, all these students are more or less the same age – somewhere between 17 and 18. Wouldn't it be more useful to find out whether they are 1st years or 2nd years – that is, how used they are to the course? This would then allow you to see whether there was any correlation between the year they're in and their attitude to the course. This could be useful.
- Q7: Demographic information is useful if you're going to be looking for correlations; but you'll definitely need to re-phrase this. Tick boxes for <u>gender</u> would be better.
- Q8: Again, you've limited the choice of answers here. You've made the assumption that the learner or their parents have made the decision. What if it was the college itself, wanting to fill up a course? Or what if they're here as a result of careers advice, or because a friend's doing the course? You've let your own assumptions limit the range of data again, so you've created a built-in bias. And one of your assumptions is that all your learners are cared for by their parents. You need to be careful not to think like this in stereotypes.

- Q9: Leaving this as a simple yes/no question won't tell you anything very useful. Wouldn't it be better to ask something like: Is there anything about the course that has disappointed you?
- Q10: This assumes an affirmative answer to the previous question, and so it is a leading question – which you must try and avoid. And once again you've allowed a very limited choice of responses. It's always a good idea to include a category of 'other', and provide a space for the respondent to tell you what that 'other' is. After all, if researchers could think of every possible response beforehand, they'd never learn anything new, would they?

I don't want you to feel too downhearted by this feedback, because at least you've made a start. But I do get the feeling that this questionnaire has been designed rather hastily. It really is worthwhile taking your time over questionnaire design. Two important things you should always keep in mind for each question are: 1) How will the responses to this help me to answer my research question? And 2) How am I going to analyse those responses? You need to make sure that every question serves a purpose and that you have the required skills and resources to analyse the data each produces.

Discussion (cont.)

There's at least one important point that the tutor doesn't raise here, and I'm not sure why. Looking at Ashraf's question objectively, we must allow for the possibility that his learners' lack of enthusiasm may have something to do with his teaching. If this is the case, would it show up in the responses to the questionnaire? Well, almost certainly no. This is because the design of the questionnaire excludes the possibility of such a finding. The questions have been formulated to accommodate the researcher's own preconceptions, and do not allow for the possibility that the answer to his research question might be an unexpected one; one that he has not envisaged because he thinks he has the answer already. He assumes any learner on a Performing Arts course should be aiming at a career in that vocational area; and that the learners' lack of motivation is their own fault. This view has driven his questionnaire design.

The lesson we can learn here is that a questionnaire should be designed with a view to *gathering answers we may not even have thought of*. We can imagine it as a fishing net. Ashraf's net has such wide holes in it that he's unlikely to catch much at all. Carefully thought out questions, like a tighter mesh, can haul in all sorts of unexpected answers; and that is what makes research so interesting.

Closed questions and open questions

Closed questions typically require only one word or very short phrase or a tick in a box for an answer. They include yes/no questions; multiple choice questions; questions that ask your age, your gender, your length of teaching experience and so on. They elicit data which can be counted, measured or otherwise analysed relatively easily and presented, if necessary in terms of numbers.

Open questions typically require a more complex answer which is expressed in the participant's own words. They are often 'Why' or 'How' questions and, because they may provoke a wide range of answers, the data they generate cannot simply be counted and will therefore be less straightforward to analyse than closed question data. However, open questions can potentially provide the rich and complex data which will bring your research alive. Ashraf's questions 3 and 5 are attempts at open questioning, but unfortunately they are not very productively worded, as his tutor has pointed out; and he has barely allowed space for a response.

Leading questions

The tutor points out that Ashraf has asked a *leading question* at the end of his questionnaire. His question is: *What would you rather be doing?* It assumes – takes for granted – that the learner would rather be doing something else other than Performing Arts. We refer to this as a 'leading question' because it leads or prompts the participant towards a particular type of response. Consider for a moment: What if the participant is perfectly content? How can their view be expressed within the context of this question? The response of 'Nothing' is not an option, and would be in any case an ambiguous answer. The problem that Ashraf has created here is that *all responses to this question will imply that the respondents would rather not be studying Performing Arts*. He is building a bias into the questionnaire because of his own assumptions. The findings of his research will therefore be flawed because they will rest on faulty evidence.

CLOSE FOCUS CLOSE FOCUS CLOSE FOCUS CLOSE FOCUS CLOSE FOCUS

Now look at the questions below. Two of them could be seen as *leading* or *prompting* questions. Can you identify which these are?
1. Do you think Performing Arts is an easy option?   Yes   No
2. When you have completed the course, do you intend to aim for a career in Performing Arts?   Yes   No   Don't know
3. Do you prefer a) practical session; or b) theory sessions?
4. Which of the following causes you to be late for lessons? a) transport problems; b) oversleeping; c) other
5. Did your school offer Performing Arts as an option in Y12?   Yes   No

TASK TASK TASK TASK **TASK** TASK TASK **TASK** TASK

Now, bearing in mind what we've learnt from analysing Ashraf's attempt at questionnaire design, let's have a look at a questionnaire produced by Chantal, a trainee-teacher working in Basic Skills. She wants to discover how mentoring within the department could be more effectively organised. Her own experience of being mentored in FE has not been a happy one, and she's hoping she can make a case for bringing about some changes. As you read through her questionnaire, make a note of anything you consider to be a strength, and also of anything you would advise her to look at again.

Questionnaire: Mentoring in the Basic Skills Department
The purpose of this questionnaire is to gather data towards an evaluation of the mentoring system within this department. The evaluation will form part of my research project for my professional qualification, and will also be submitted as a report to the Head of Department. The questionnaires are designed to be completed anonymously, so that no responses can be traced back to any named individual.

Please indicate your answer by ticking the appropriate option.
1. Have you ever been mentored?   Yes   No
2. If you answered 'yes', were you given a choice about your mentor?   Yes   No

---

3. If you answered 'yes' to Question 1, was it in this department?   Yes   No
4. Have you ever been a mentor?   Yes   No
5. If you answered 'yes', were you given a choice about whom you mentored?   Yes   No
6. If you answered 'yes' to Question 4, was it in this department?   Yes   No
7. If you have been a mentor in the past, did you receive any training for the role?   Yes No
8. If you have been mentored in this department, did you find the experience:
   not useful_____fairly useful_____mostly useful _____very useful
9. Are you: male female
10. What is your age group? Under 25   25–35   36–46   47–57   58–65
11. How long have you taught? Less than 5 yrs   5–10yrs   11–25yrs   over 25yrs

For each of the following questions, please write your response in the box provided.
12. In your view, what is the purpose of mentoring?

13. What sort of mentor support would you find most useful at this stage of your career?

14. If you have personal experience of mentoring or being mentored *outside* this department please describe it briefly here:

15. If you have personal experience of mentoring or being mentored *inside* this department please describe it briefly here:

Thank you for completing this questionnaire.

Discussion

You'll have noticed that Chantal's questionnaire has a number of strengths that Ashraf's lacked. First, the information for participants with which it begins is explicit about the purpose and scope of her research and correctly promises anonymity. Anyone completing it, therefore, is implicitly giving their informed consent to participate in the research. Second, she provides clear instructions to respondents about how to indicate their answers. Third, for questions that require more than a 'yes or no' answer, she does not limit the choice of response to a narrow range determined by her own preconceptions, but provides space for open answers. This creates the possibility of capturing unexpected or unpredicted data. The one exception to this is where she asks about the usefulness of being mentored. Here she provides a scale on which the participant can indicate the degree of usefulness. This means of capturing and measuring a response is known as a *Likert scale.* One of its advantages to the researcher is that it enables straightforward analysis of results. For example, Chantal could say, 'Seven out of twelve participants responded that their experience of being mentored was fairly useful.' Or she could present the findings from this question as a block graph. One decision she has had to take, in using this form of scaled response, is how many possible answers to include in the scale. She has chosen to present an even number. This means that there is no 'middle' response which would allow the respondent to simply sit on the fence. Also, she has chosen a scale of descriptors, rather than a numbered continuum where, for example, 1 would indicate not useful and 4 would indicate most useful. Perhaps she considers that using descriptors will leave less room for error or misunderstanding. Whatever her reasons, we can see her use of a scale here as a type of multiple choice question which will produce the data she needs. If she had approached this aspect of her inquiry as an open question, on the other hand, she would have been faced with a dozen or so discursive answers which she would then have had to analyse, categorise and summarise before she could present them as findings.

This is exactly what she will have to do with the open questions that form the second half of her questionnaire. But in this case she may feel it worth the effort, since open questions are the best way to elicit the specific data about participants' views and experiences that she is seeking here. Dividing the questionnaire into two sections, first closed questions and then open ones, is an interesting approach and Chantal's intention here may be to encourage participation and completion by beginning with questions which are quick and easy to answer, and only then progressing to ones whose answers need a bit more thought and effort. You'll also note that she has kept the questionnaire fairly brief. This will also improve the chances of completion and return.

Her choice of questions, and the combination of open and closed, will provide her with a variety of opportunities for correlation. For example, she can correlate participants' views and experiences by age, by gender, by length of teaching experience, by whether or not they have mentored or been mentored within the department, or any combination of these. She can interrogate the data in all sorts of ways; for example, to discover whether the mentoring experiences of older women with less than five years' teaching experience differ from those of young men also fairly new to the profession. Or she could look at whether participants with high expectations of mentoring are also those whose experiences have been positive; and so on. In other words, she has designed the questionnaire with due attention not only to what sort of data she needs, but also to how she eventually intends to analyse that data when the questionnaires are completed and returned.

CLOSE FOCUS CLOSE FOCUS CLOSE FOCUS CLOSE FOCUS CLOSE FOCUS

Chantal had a particular view of mentoring within her department. She thought there should be some changes. Has this shown up as bias anywhere in her questionnaire? For example, does she use any leading questions?

Focus groups

Like questionnaires, the focus group is a method which allows the researcher to gather data from groups of participants in a time-effective way. One way to picture it is as a sort of group interview, where the researcher might start off the discussion by putting a question to the group and then noting the comments and discussion that ensue. The proceedings can be tightly structured, with the researcher firmly in control and a list of questions to be got through; or it can be fairly open, with the researcher initially tabling the discussion topic and then sitting back. The approach will depend very much on the research question and the researcher's aims and style. Some researchers use multiple focus groups; others may use just one. The size of group may be very small – just three or four participants – or quite large; but it should never be so large as to prevent a productive and inclusive discussion.

By its very nature the focus group is particularly useful for maintaining participants' anonymity because the data it provides is treated as the product of the group and not of individuals within that group. For the researcher who needs to collect data from vulnerable groups, such as learners under the age of 16, the focus group is an ideal method to use for this reason. And, of course, the security provided by being part of a group can make participants – particularly younger ones – feel more confident about contributing their views and becoming part of the group's collective voice.

Below you will see Table 6.1 showing a comparison between the use of questionnaires and focus groups as methods for gathering data. It is the researcher's task to decide which method best suits their purpose. Or they may decide, as Chantal does, to use both.

Table 6.1 Comparing the uses and usefulness of questionnaires and focus groups

Questionnaires	Focus groups
No limits on number of participants (other than what's practical in terms of time needed for analysis)	Limits number of participants because too many will make productive discussion impossible
Easy to maintain participants' anonymity	Easy to maintain participants' anonymity
Questions have to stand alone. No opportunity for exploration or clarification	Plenty of opportunity to explore answers further and to clarify questions
Can yield poor completion rate	Discussion encourages engagement
Usually completed individually. No opportunity for respondents to 'bounce' ideas	Group discussion can generate and explore new ideas.
The leading nature of questions may go unnoticed, resulting in biased data	Confidence arising from strength of numbers means more possibility that leading questions and researcher assumptions may be challenged
Can be designed so that data is easy to analyse	The process of data analysis is much more complex
Can yield both quantitative and qualitative data	Normally used to generate qualitative data only
Suitable for closed questions	Ideal for the discussion of open questions
All participants able to voice views	Quiet or shy participants' voices may be excluded or unheard

Chantal's focus group

In order to find out whether there is any important data which her questionnaire has failed to pick up, Chantal decides to introduce some *methodological triangulation* into her research and hold a focus group which will take as its starting point one of the open questions in her questionnaire: *'In your view, what is the purpose of mentoring?'* Nine colleagues from the Basic Skills department volunteer to take part, having given informed consent for the discussion to be audio recorded and having been promised anonymity in the written report. They meet at 5 p.m. in one of the classrooms. You can read the transcript of part of their discussion below.

TASK TASK **TASK** TASK **TASK TASK** TASK **TASK** TASK **TASK TASK** TASK

As you read the extract from the focus group transcript, make a note of:

- **what other questions are being answered, if any;**
- **what difficulties the analysis of focus group data might present to the researcher;**
- **what ethical issues arise here, and how Chantal should address them.**

Focus group transcript January 23rd

C: Okay, folks. Well I'd like to get your view first of all on what you think the purpose of mentoring is.

– Support.

– Yes, it's about support, isn't it. It's about...

– It's not just about support, though, is it? It's about making sure someone's doing their job properly. It's about keeping an eye on them.

– Well, it is in this place.

Laughter

– It's an assessment role, really, isn't it? The mentor assesses your teaching and tells you what you're doing wrong and...

– Yes, but it's not supposed to be like that. Mentoring. Mentoring's supposed to be about supporting professional development. When I was working in the health service...

– Explaining to someone what they're not doing right does support professional development, surely? I mean...

– But there are ways of doing it, aren't there? You know. I mean, you can encourage someone to reflect on how they've been teaching and help them to plan what they'd like to change or what they need to change. Or you can sit them down and tell them what they're doing wrong. Which is the way it seems to work in this place.

More laughter

– But that's the trouble, though, isn't it? Mentoring sounds all warm and fluffy, like you're going to be looked after and supported and that. And then it turns out it's a big stick to hit you with and you end up feeling crap about yourself and your teaching.

– It's not only that, though. I think it runs like a sort of informant system, don't you? An informant system. You know, where the mentor keeps an eye on what you're doing and then runs back and tells the boss. It does, doesn't it, though?

– Foucault. Surveillance. It's...

– But it's not like that everywhere. When I was working in the health service...

- We collude, though, don't we? When I'm mentoring someone I fill in all the forms, and I try to be supportive about the way I do it. But I don't get any time allowance, so what am I supposed to do? There's no time for long heart-to-hearts and action planning. It's just wham, here's your assessment, thank you very much, and here's a copy for the boss.
- If there's no time allowed for it, we should just say we're not going to do it.
- You've got to be kidding!
- No one says no to her and lives.
  More laughter

Discussion

You'll see that Chantal takes a quite unstructured approach. She asks her question and then sits back. One advantage of this is that there is no risk of her introducing her own bias and participants are given free rein while she waits and listens to hear what emerges. In fact the group of its own accord very quickly moves on to a different question, but one which was also included in the questionnaire: *'If you have personal experience of mentoring or being mentored inside this department please describe it briefly here'.* Chantal could justifiably conclude from this that mentoring in the department is a topic which is of concern to them; and she will probably include this observation as part of her findings when she writes up her report.

This transcript of the recording also captures very vividly some of the difficulties focus groups can present to the researcher. The chief one is that informal discussion can look chaotic on the page. People interrupt. Most people don't get to finish their sentences. And because speakers cannot be identified it is almost impossible to follow any individual's train of thought or argument. There are frustrations, too. Someone in the group (we assume it is one person) is trying to say something about their experience of mentoring in the health service. This could be useful to the researcher, but the participant never gets to finish their sentence. And someone else is trying to make a point about Foucault and surveillance, which might provide Chantal with an interesting theoretical perspective; but this is not an interview, and so this thread, too, is lost. What she must do as researcher is to categorise the themes that are emerging from this discussion. She must listen for the voice of the group, not for individuals within it.

And finally, there are ethical issues here, which Chantal must consider. First, there is the possibility that what she is doing in facilitating this discussion could be interpreted as encouraging criticism of people and practices within the department, which could leave her open to an accusation of being unprofessional. So she will need to handle this situation very carefully and make sure her choice of further questions avoids escalating the mood of complaint. Second, she now finds herself in possession of data which is highly critical of someone – presumably the department head. She will have to decide now whether anonymity (of the focus group membership, the department, the department head) will be sufficient here, or whether she should keep these particular snippets of data confidential and not include them in her report at all.

Branching options

You may like to choose one of the following activities which are designed to help you apply what you've learnt from this chapter to your own practice. The first encourages you, as a professional, to develop your skills of reflection; the second asks you to take an evaluative approach consistent with an initial teaching qualification in the sector; and the third is designed to support skills of critical analysis appropriate to post-qualification CPD or Masters level study.

Reflection

Re-write Ashraf's questionnaire in response to his tutor's feedback, and also incorporate any other improvements you think may be necessary.

Evaluation

We have seen how Chantal's questionnaire design will allow her to look for correlations between various data. Now have a look at Ashraf's questionnaire again and see what correlations he will be able to look for. How useful will these be in answering his research question?

Critical analysis

1. Chantal combines two methods in order to include methodological triangulation. However, she does not use data triangulation in her questionnaire. What question or questions could she add in order to do this?

2. We know that, in writing up her findings from the focus group, Chantal must listen for and report on the voice of the group, not individuals within it. How would you summarise the view of the group? Draft a paragraph for Chantal's research report, setting this out.

REFERENCES AND FURTHER READING REFERENCES AND FURTHER READING

If you would like to read more, the following two books provide useful and straightforward chapters on using questionnaires and focus groups in educational research, although they do not use a specifically FE context:

Cohen, L., Manion, L. and Morrison, K. (2011) *Research Methods in Education* (7th edition). London: Routledge.

Wellington, J. (2000) *Educational Research: Contemporary Issues and Practical Approaches*. London: Continuum.

7
Watching and listening: observations and interviews

The objectives of this chapter

This chapter will look at the practicalities of setting up observations and interviews. It will discuss the purposes, benefits and potential difficulties of these two popular approaches to gathering educational research data in an FE setting. We'll be exploring ways to record the data collected via these methods, and the potential impact of power relationships on what we see and hear.

The chapter will revisit some key research terminology as well as introducing some which may be new or unfamiliar, such as: *respondent; informant; loaded questions; complex questions; interview schedule; transcriptions; interrogation of data; trustworthiness of data.*

Introduction

Interviews

There are good reasons why interviewing is such a widely used method of research in education. It allows the researcher to interact with participants individually in a dialogue which makes it possible to probe questions further, seek clarification, re-phrase questions and so on. It also provides the opportunity for the researcher to put the participant at ease and encourage them to speak honestly and confidently. Interviews can be used to gather a range of data from straightforward facts about people's life histories, to their opinions and assumptions. They can even be used to explore what we can learn about participants' values and beliefs from the language they use to express themselves. What is sometimes forgotten, though, is that interviewing has its disadvantages, too. What is said must be recorded somehow, and then transcribed and analysed, which can be very time-consuming. At the same time, there will be *epistemological* questions raised. In what sense is what someone says in an interview a sound basis for constructing 'knowledge'? The researcher will need to consider the *trustworthiness* of the data: How can they know whether what the interviewee has said is 'true'? Could their responses have been influenced by the power relationship between interviewer and interviewee? And the resulting qualitative data must then be interrogated and interpreted by the researcher – a process which is always vulnerable to researcher bias. So, interviews are by no means an easy option. As you read on through this chapter, you will be able to decide for yourself whether, for your purposes, their advantages outweigh their disadvantages.

Observations

Like interviews, observations have the advantage that they bring the researcher and participant/s face to face and allow the researcher to make first-hand judgements about what they hear and see. They can offer a high level of validity. If you want to research what is happening, the best way, if it's at all practical, is to go and see for yourself. This may often be more useful than, for example, simply asking someone about it. Observations will not provide you with bias-free data, because you will inevitably be looking at what you observe through your own preconceptions and values. But careful reflection may help you to become aware of your own bias as observer; whereas, if you rely instead on second-hand or witness accounts, you risk their unknown (and possibly unknowable) bias being incorporated into your findings. However, observation data, like interview data, may be rendered unreliable because of the power relations between observer and observed. For example, if you, as researcher, hold a senior position in relation to the participant, they may be intimidated by your presence to an extent where what you observe is not what would have taken place if you had not been there. It is axiomatic that the very presence of the observer, however unobtrusive, changes what is observed because it introduces a change into the environment or the context. Observations, therefore, always require us to consider the issue of reliability. We'll be exploring all these aspects in more detail as the chapter progresses.

Patience interviews employers

Patience is interested in learners' progression to work. She has been teaching in FE for two years, and it is her view that vocational education and training are meaningless if it does not result in trainees gaining employment on successful completion. However, she has seen that progression to employment figures have been quite low for her department for the past three years, and she has begun to wonder whether there is something wrong here that should be investigated. She is required to do a research project as part of her professional development, and so she decides to use this as an opportunity to try to find out what is going on. It seems to her that the best place to start is with local employers. So she sends out emails to 13 employers explaining her project and asking for volunteers. She receives three positive responses. Now all she has to do is to draw up an interview schedule and then arrange to conduct the first interview as a pilot.

TASK TASK **TASK** TASK **TASK TASK** TASK **TASK** TASK **TASK TASK** TASK

Below is Patience's schedule of questions for the first interview. Read it through and consider the following questions:
- **What feedback would you give her on the phrasing of questions 7, 8 and 9?**
- **What feedback would you give her on the sequencing of the question?**
- **Has she built in any internal data triangulation?**
- **Is there any other point arising from this list that you would want to raise with her?**

Interviewing employers: Interview schedule
1. Can you tell me a bit about your business, when it was founded and so on?
2. How many employees do you have currently?
3. What is your policy on employing newly qualified staff?
4. What sort of qualities and skills do you look for in your employees?
5. Can you tell me a bit about the sort of vocational qualifications you value when selecting new employees?
6. How important in employees do you consider people skills such as the ability to communicate and get on with others compared to quantifiable skills such as literacy and numeracy?

---

7. To what extent do you think trainees straight from college are unprepared for the world of work?
8. What are the advantages and disadvantages of employing someone straight from college, and if faced with a choice between an applicant with previous employment experience and one who was newly qualified what would be your own preference and how much influence would you have on the final decision?
9. What is your view of some employers' rigid, and some might say rather unfair idea of requiring all new employees to have had previous relevant experience?
10. What advice would you give to an applicant applying for a post here with a good vocational qualification straight from college?

Discussion

First of all, let's clarify what we mean by *interview schedule*. It is the list of proposed questions in the order you plan to ask them. It has nothing to do with the 'scheduling' or timing of the interview as the name might at first suggest. Secondly, we've learned that Patience plans to *pilot* her interview schedule. This means she will try it out, either with one of the participants or with a colleague or other volunteer, before she continues on to the interviews she will be using for her research data. There are several good reasons why she will do this. A pilot or trial run will enable her to see whether her questions are clearly understood. It will give her an opportunity to practise her listening skills and discover whether she needs to try harder, for example, to allow the interviewee time to think about the answer or to finish their sentences. She will also be able to see whether her chosen method of recording the interview – whether that's by audio or note-taking or video or a combination of these – is practicable; and what effect it might have on the interviewee's confidence or willingness to communicate.

However, before she uses it for the pilot stage, we're going to give her some feedback on her interview schedule which may lead her to make some amendments.

- First of all, you were asked what feedback you would give her on the phrasing of questions 7, 8 and 9. You will probably have noticed that these questions are leading, over-complicated and loaded respectively. We discussed the problem of leading questions when we were looking at questionnaires in Chapter 6. When Patience asks question 7: *'To what extent do you think trainees straight from college are unprepared for the world of work?'* she is *leading* the interviewee towards an answer that trainees are *unprepared for the world of work to some extent*. What she's trying to find out here is *whether or not* the employer thinks trainees are prepared, but instead she is building a bias into the question. When she asks question 8: *'What are the advantages and disadvantages of employing someone straight from college, and if faced with a choice between an applicant with previous employment experience and one who was newly qualified what would be your own preference and how much influence would you have on the final decision?'* she is really asking four questions. Shoved altogether they create a sentence – and a query – which is so convoluted that the interviewee is likely to have forgotten the last part before they have finished answering the first. Complex or over-complicated questions should be avoided in interviews. And then there is question 9: *'What is your view of some employers' rigid, and some might say rather unfair idea of requiring all new employees to have had previous relevant experience?'* We call this a loaded question because it is weighted with the researcher's own values and opinions. It also directs the interviewee in no uncertain terms to the 'correct' answer. Given the power relationships that can exist within the context of an interview, it is particularly bad practice to word questions in a way which invites the interviewee

- to join the researcher on the high moral ground. It builds in bias and makes the data unreliable.
- So, what feedback would you give her on the sequencing of the questions? Well, on the whole she's made some good decisions here. The first question is a very open one which invites the interviewee to answer in any way that they choose and so gives them a sense of ownership over the interview process. The first few questions show no evidence of the interviewer having an 'agenda'. They simply provide an opportunity for the interviewee to talk about their business. This will have the effect of putting the interviewee at their ease before Patience hits them with the 'big' questions 5–10.
- Has she built in any internal data triangulation? Yes, you will probably have seen that she has, by covering the same or similar ground in questions 4 and 5, but each in a slightly different way. If the interviewee's answers to these two questions are consistent with one another it makes it more likely that this data is trustworthy and reliable.
- You may have found other points you would want to raise with Patience. One that I would draw her attention to is that question 2 is a closed question, and seems a waste of opportunity to use an interview with all its potential for gathering complex, nuanced data, to ask a question which requires only a one-word answer. Perhaps she should instead have requested this sort of baseline information at an earlier stage when asking for volunteers. She would then appear better prepared at interview if she can quote this figure herself.

CLOSE FOCUS CLOSE FOCUS CLOSE FOCUS CLOSE FOCUS

Reword Patience's questions 7, 8 and 9 so that they are not loaded, leading or over-complicated.

Conducting the interview

So, Patience has now amended her interview schedule in response to our comments and advice, and she is ready to conduct the pilot interview. She chooses to do this with one of her three volunteer employers as she will then be able to incorporate the data into her research and this will save her time.

TASK TASK TASK TASK TASK TASK TASK TASK

Below is a transcript of the interview. Read it carefully and make a note of any comments or questions you have.

Interview 1. Pilot interview. Transcript

P: Thank you for agreeing to be interviewed. Do you mind if I use this voice recorder? It'll be easier than trying to take notes. And I don't want to miss anything important.

Empl: Go ahead. That's fine by me.

P: Thank you. I just... There, that's it. So, can you tell me a bit about your business, when it was founded and so on?

Empl: Well, we started up in 2003 with six people on the payroll, and it's taken off from there, really. We've got 23 staff here now, and last year we opened up another office in the north of the county where we've got eight on payroll and looking to expand a bit there next year.

P: So you'll be taking new people on?

Empl: We're hoping so. Yeah.

P: And so what's your policy on employing newly qualified staff?

Empl: What do you mean?

P: Well...

Empl: We take people on when it becomes obvious that existing personnel have got too much volume of work to cope with. But we're always quite cautious about it, because what we don't want to do is take people on and then let them go. That's no help to them or us. We're only a small outfit and we have to balance expansion with caution because we have a responsibility to the people who're employed here.

P: Okay, so what sort of qualities and skills do you look for in your employees?

Empl: Well that depends what we're taking them on to do, doesn't it? [Laughs] Like, we don't need them to have a clean driving licence if they're here to do the invoicing, but we do if they're here to take the vans out.

P: But are there any sort of, you know, personal qualities you'd be looking for?

Empl: Hard workers. Honesty. Good sense of humour [Laughs]. There's things you can't tell about a person until they've been working for you for a bit. That's the trouble.

P: Alright then. What sort of vocational qualifications do you value when you're selecting new employees?

Empl: Well obviously we want them to have qualifications that are relevant to the job. Do you mean what level, that sort of thing?

P: Er, yes. If you like...

Empl: If I like? It's you doing the interviewing [Laughs]. To be honest, we put much more weight on references. Some of these vocational qualifications are ten a penny, aren't they? You get youngsters coming along with their bits of paper but they've no idea. No idea at all.

P: So are you saying that you favour applicants with previous experience over newly qualified applicants?

Empl: Every time [Laughs].

P: But that's not very fair, is it? I mean, how are they going to get experience if...

Empl: Hang on a minute. I'm not a charity, you know. We're not running a charity here. We're running a business. Here I am giving up my time to talk to you and then you start lecturing me. I think we've about got to the end of this, thank you very much My receptionist'll show you out.

Discussion

Oh dear. That didn't go too well. And, as a consequence, Patience didn't get the opportunity to ask her last four questions, which were perhaps the most important ones on her list. So what can she learn about interviewing skills from this experience? Her mentor has gone through the transcript to advise her on where and how this all went wrong and whether she can salvage anything useful from the interview. He's returned the transcript to her with tracked comments. Let's have a look at what he's said. As you read his comments, compare them to your own notes.

Interview 1. Pilot interview. Transcript

P: Thank you for agreeing to be interviewed. Do you mind if I use this voice recorder? It'll be easier than trying to take notes. And I don't want to miss anything important.

Empl: Go ahead. That's fine by me.

P: Thank you. I just... There, that's it. So, can you tell me a bit about your business, when it was founded and so on?

Empl: Well, we started up in 2003 with six people on the payroll, and it's taken off from there, really. We've got 23 staff here now, and last year we opened up another office in the north of the county where we've got eight on payroll and looking to expand a bit there next year.

Comment [S1]: A good way to start.

Comment [S2]: Good. It's important to ask permission.

Comment [S3]: This is useful background information that you could use when looking for correlations between – for example – the size or age of a business and its attitudes towards employing college leavers.

P: So you'll be taking new people on?

Empl: We're hoping so. Yeah.

P: And so what's your policy on employing newly qualified staff?

Empl: What do you mean?

P: Well...

Empl: We take people on when we it becomes obvious that existing personnel have got too much volume of work to cope with. But we're always quite cautious about it, because what we don't want to do is take people on and then let them go. That's no help to them or us. We're only a small outfit and we have to balance expansion with caution because we have a responsibility to the people who're been employed here.

P: Okay, so what sort of qualities and skills do you look for in your employees?

Empl: Well that depends what we're taking them on to do, doesn't it? [Laughs] Like, we don't need them to have a clean driving licence if they're here to do the invoicing, but we do if they're here to take the vans out.

P: But are there any sort of, you know, personal qualities you'd be looking for?

Empl: Hard workers. Honesty. Good sense of humour [Laughs]. There's things you can't tell about a person until they've working for you for a bit. That's the trouble.

P: Alright then. What sort of vocational qualifications do you value when you're selecting new employees?

Empl: Well obviously we want them to have qualifications that are relevant to the job. Do you mean what level, that sort of thing?

P: Er, yes. If you like...

Empl: If I like? It's you doing the interviewing [Laughs]. To be honest, we put much more weight on references. Some of these vocational qualifications are ten a penny, aren't they? You get youngsters coming along with their bits of paper but they've no idea. No idea at all.

P: So are you saying that you favour applicants with previous experience over newly qualified applicants?

Empl: Every time [Laughs].

P: But that's not very fair, is it? I mean, how are they going to get experience if...

Empl: Hang on a minute. I'm not a charity, you know. We're not running a charity here. We're running a business. Here I am giving up my time to talk to you and then you start lecturing me. I think we've about got to the end of this, thank you very much My receptionist'll show you out.

Comment [S4]: You deviate here from your interview schedule. Is this for clarification, or are you letting your role as tutor interfere with your role as researcher here?

Comment [S5]: Your interviewee seeks clarification here. This is an example of how a pilot interview can be useful. You may want to think again about how to phrase this question to make its purpose clearer.

Comment [S6]: Good! You turned this into a specific question in order to get a useful response. You would still have been able to use this for internal triangulation if you'd not lost the opportunity to ask your last few questions!

Comment [S7]: This may explain the employer's preference for selecting applicants who have previous experience and can therefore provide references. You could have explored this possibility instead of ploughing on with your next question. The opportunity for explorations is one of the advantages of interviews and you've missed this here.

Comment [S8]: Again, there's an indication here that the question doesn't work very well in practice and may need re-phrasing.

Comment [S9]: You lose the initiative here. But also you're giving the interviewee an opportunity to lead the agenda – which can be useful.

Comment [S10]: Instead of treating this as valuable data, you allow it to rattle you, as becomes apparent by your final remark. If you allow your own views to influence the interview dialogue you are introducing bias into your research – as well as risking offending your interviewee!

Comment [S11]: This is a leading question, and also sounds like a criticism. There are other ways to phrase this. You've deviated from your list of questions here, with unfortunate results.

Deviation

The mentor makes the point that one reason interviews are very useful is that they allow the researcher to seek immediate clarification or probe particularly interesting responses which is impossible to do in questionnaires. It's perfectly acceptable, therefore, to not stick rigidly to your prepared list of questions if deviation here and there will enrich or clarify the data.

Perhaps it is clarification that Patience is seeking when she asks whether the business will be taking people on. But what she seems to do, though, towards the end, is to deviate from her schedule of questions in order to enter into an argument with her interviewee. She abandons her research role in order to leap to the defence of her learners, and so unfortunately her opportunity to take the interview further is lost.

Hesitations, laughter and body language

Patience's interview transcript captures the interviewee's laughter. But it doesn't record the 'ums' and 'ers', nor the body language adopted by the interviewee, and yet both these things are communication of a sort. They can tell us how sure someone is of their answer, or if they are feeling nervous, or even whether they are giving a truthful response. Some researchers will include these types of 'communication' in their transcripts and will take them into consideration when analysing the data. Interpreting hesitations, gestures, verbal tics and so on can never be an exact science. For example, what does this employer's occasional laughter signify, in your view? Including these factors in an analysis of the interview data increases the risk of introducing researcher bias. You might think the laughter shows the employer to be a jovial bloke; I might think it means he's hiding something.

Respondent or informant

Patience drew up a structured list of questions to which she sought interviewees' response. She's chosen an approach to interviewing in which the researcher controls the agenda and the interviewee has the role of *respondent* (Powney and Watts, 1987). But there is an alternative approach, in which the interviewer asks a general, open question centred on their research topic, and then encourages the interviewee to take this in whatever direction they choose. This type of interview is what Powney and Watts (1987) refer to as an *informant* interview. It allows participants to reveal their own agenda and is more likely to provide data that the researcher could not or did not predict than a rigid set of researcher-led questions and answers. Whether to use a respondent or informant style interview – or a combination of the two – is one of the decisions the researcher will need to make.

Recording the interview

Another important decision is about how the interview should be recorded. Patience chooses an audio recording device. This will provide her with an accurate record of the interview (although, as we've seen, there are some important aspects it cannot capture, such as body language). It will also, unlike note-taking, allow her to maintain eye contact with the interviewee, an important factor in encouraging their input. You can test this for yourself by imagining talking to someone who looks away from you most of the time. It can be very disconcerting. And audio recording is usually considered to be less intrusive than video recording, which can make the interviewee too self-conscious to talk freely. So Patience has made a good choice here, in terms of accuracy and keeping up the interview flow. Although audio recordings are time-consuming to transcribe, it is not always necessary to transcribe the whole thing as Patience has done. Sometimes it is sufficient to transcribe only those extracts you plan to quote in your research report, and to summarise the main points of the rest.

Trustworthiness and reliability

Finally, it's important to consider how much we can trust data collected by interview. One of the obvious questions we have to ask ourselves is: 'Was the interviewee telling the truth?' This is about the *trustworthiness* of the data. There are all kinds of reasons why participants' responses may be inaccurate. They may themselves be ill-informed or mistaken. They may aim to please us by giving the answer they think we want to hear. They may feel intimidated because of an imbalance of power in their relationship with you, and so feel they have to give you the 'correct' answer. Or they may believe they have answered openly and honestly, but be unconsciously deceiving themselves in this. The bottom line is that we can never be 100 per cent certain that our interview data is trustworthy. The way we deal with this is to acknowledge this uncertainty when we write up our research report. If we demonstrate that we are alert to the possibility that our data cannot be treated as incontrovertible 'fact' and that we have taken what measures we can to ensure that it is as trustworthy as we can make it, that will be the best that we, as researchers, can do.

Reliability is also an issue with interview data. How can we know whether the interviewee would respond in the same way if interviewed on a different day or by a different researcher? Might one researcher's interview style succeed in encouraging a participant to answer in detail while another might cause them to 'clam up'? We can see from Patience's interview how the skill or attitude of the researcher can affect the conduct of the interview. A different researcher using Patience's list of questions might have collected more detailed, or even different, responses.

What we've been discussing here is the question of whether data is 'true'. *Truth* is a slippery word in the context of research, and one which we must use with caution. Our understandings or beliefs about what constitutes *knowing* or *truth* are something we need to explain in our research report. They are part of the *epistemological* context which underlies our choice of research method.

CLOSE FOCUS CLOSE FOCUS **CLOSE FOCUS** CLOSE FOCUS **CLOSE FOCUS**

Which of the following questions would be an indicator of an informant style interview?
- **What does your role in the business involve?**
- **How is a job specification drawn up?**
- **Talk me through your recruitment and employment processes.**

Observation

As mentioned at the beginning of this chapter, doing observations as part of your research project carries some of the same problems with reliability as the interview. For example, observation data will be unreliable if the power relations between observer and observed causes the person or people observed to behave in a way which is not representative of their normal practice. And reliability is inevitably affected by the very presence of an observer. These are fairly recognisable drawbacks. But a less obvious problem is that you will always be looking at what you observe through a prism of your own preconceptions and values. A useful way to think about this is to imagine the data – that which you are observing – as a stream of light which is intercepted by you, the observer. But you are not transparent. So that stream of data cannot flow straight through you and on to the page of the report unaltered. It is always mediated by you. It is like light shining through coloured glass. It will take on the colours of that glass as it emerges on the other side, tinted by your own values and attitudes. It's important, therefore, not to assume that observation is somehow more 'objective' than other methods. But it does have the advantage that it can offer a high level of *validity*.

TASK TASK **TASK** TASK **TASK** **TASK** TASK **TASK** TASK **TASK** **TASK** TASK

Patience decides to follow up her interviews by sitting in and observing some of her learners have a session of mock job interviews with two local employers who have volunteered to engage in this simulation and then provide learners with individual feedback. Under the heading *'Method'* she writes up her *use* of observation; and under the heading *'Methodology'* she explains the *advantages and disadvantages* of this method and her *reasons for choosing it*. These will form part of her final research report. You will find this extract below. As you read it through, look out particularly for how she has a) justified her choice of method; and b) also demonstrated that she is aware of its disadvantages.

Method

As well as conducting interviews, I also observed a session in college where learners were given the opportunity to take part in simulated job interviews conducted by real employers who then gave feedback and offered advice. Having obtained informed consent from all those involved, I arranged to sit at the back of the room, out of the sight line of interviewer and interviewee but with a clear view of what was happening. I used a pre-prepared sheet for each 'applicant' on which I had printed a series of scales numbered 1 to 10 on which to score applicants' confidence, audibility, social skills, knowledge of the vocational area, and body language. This data allowed me to compare my own estimate of their performance with the interviewer's feedback in order to discover whether the advice learners are receiving from myself and the team is consistent with what employers are looking for. This would help me to answer my research question which is about why our learners' progression rates to paid employment in a relevant vocational sector have recently been poorer than expected.

Methodology

One advantage of using observation in this context is that it allows me to see at first hand how our learners might perform at interview and how local employers rate them as potential employees based on that interview performance. It also provided me with an opportunity for methodological triangulation because I could now compare what employers told me in the interviews that they were looking for in new employees, and what it was apparent they were looking for from their feedback from these simulated interviews. Triangulation is one way of checking the reliability and trustworthiness of data. This was particularly important here, since observations, like interviews, are vulnerable to accusations of producing unreliable data. As an observer, my very presence in that environment would have some impact on what I was observing. And the record of my observation as noted on the scales I used was inevitably a subjective one. When assessing the level of social skills each learner exhibited, for example, I was making a judgement based on my own values and assumptions. Another observer might have scored these differently. However, as there was only one observer – myself – the judgement behind the scoring was consistent. And it was, after all, the judgement of myself (and the team) which I wished to compare to the judgement of the employers. While acknowledging, therefore, the limited reliability of the raw data in the form of the scores, this comparison was a useful one and the observation was a valid means to explore it.

A SUMMARY OF **KEY POINTS**

In this chapter we have discussed:

> **planning and conducting interviews;**

> **the distinction between respondent interviews and informant interviews;**

> **some pitfalls of interviewing, and how they can be avoided;**

> **advantages and difficulties of collecting data through observations;**

> **evaluating the trustworthiness and reliability of interview and observation data.**

We have also identified some useful terms to use when writing about interviews and observations. These include: *respondent; informant; loaded questions; complex questions; interview schedule; transcriptions; interrogation of data; trustworthiness of data.*

Branching options

You may like to choose one of the following activities which are designed to help you apply what you've learnt from this chapter to your own practice. The first encourages you, as a professional, to develop your skills of reflection; the second asks you to take an evaluative approach consistent with an initial teaching qualification in the sector; and the third is designed to support skills of critical analysis appropriate to post-qualification CPD or Masters level study.

Reflection

What else might Patience have usefully looked for in her observation of the job interview simulations which would have helped her to answer her research question?

Evaluation

Evaluate: a) the reliability; and b) the validity of Patience's data from her pilot interview, giving reasons and examples to support your argument.

Critical analysis

You have seen how Patience writes up her methodological justification for using observations as a research method. Using this as a template, draft for her the section of her report which will explain and justify her use of interviews.

REFERENCES AND FURTHER READING

When referring to 'informant' and 'respondent' interviews, this chapter refers to the following work which is, unfortunately, currently out of print. Used copies are available through the internet:

Powney, J. and Watts, M. (1987) *Interviewing in Educational Research.* London: Routledge and Kegan Paul.

You will also find useful chapters on interviewing and observations in:

Cohen, L., Manion, L. and Morrison, K. (2011) *Research Methods in Education* (7th edition). London: Routledge.

Wellington, J. (2000) *Educational Research: Contemporary Issues and Practical Approaches*. London: Continuum.

8
Paper chase: exploring policies and other documents

The objectives of this chapter

This chapter will focus on documentary research and particularly on the analysis of policy documents, ways in which their underlying assumptions can be identified, and their potential impact evaluated. It will look at how national policy documents relating to FE can be subjected to a critical analysis; and also how institutional policies – for example on anti-bullying or inclusion – can be made the subject of useful and interesting research.

The chapter will revisit some key research terminology, such as *desktop research,* as well as introducing some which may be new or unfamiliar, such as: *policy archeology; policy analysis; discourse; discourse analysis; polemic; ideology; textual analysis; rhetoric.*

Introduction

So far we have been looking at methods of investigation which involve us in finding things out about *people*: listening to them, or directly observing them, or engaging with them through questionnaires. All of these approaches are to a greater or lesser extent participative; that is, they require the inclusion of research participants. In this chapter we're going to be looking at a method of research that doesn't necessarily involve us in direct interaction with other people at all. In fact, we can carry it out for the most part simply sitting at a desk with our computer and whatever hard copy documents we need. This is why it is sometimes called *desktop research*. Some research questions are best suited to this approach, and so we should consider it just as useful as the interactive and people-centred research we've been looking at so far.

Imagine for a moment that you are investigating your family tree. If you want to discover information about your parents' or your grandparents' generation there will be people around whom you can ask. You may interview them. You may even ask them to fill in questionnaires. You may observe their behaviour, their manners, their way of doing things – all of which will give you an understanding of the lives of those generations. But if you wanted to find out personal details about your great, great, great grandparents, your main sources of data would be documents: birth, marriage and death certificates; census details; army records; wills; diaries; letters and so on. Here, documentary or desktop research could suit your purpose best. In the same way, a researcher in FE may formulate a research question which requires recourse to documentary evidence – rather than what people might say or do – as the most reliable source of valid data.

Arnold does some desktop research

Take, for example, Arnold's research question. He has been interested to hear of government proposals to raise the status of vocational qualifications and to encourage people to value them equally with 'academic' qualifications such as A levels. But he has a feeling that he has heard all this before. Is this a case of déjà vu, or has this promise of parity been made repeatedly in the past to little effect? He decides to do some research into government policy statements about vocational qualifications over the previous two decades and to submit this as the research project he's required to complete as part of his in-service professional development. His tutor advises him that a good source of data will be White Papers relating specifically to FE and vocational education and training. Arnold begins his search and sets out a first draft for his tutor to comment on.

TASK TASK TASK TASK **TASK** TASK TASK **TASK**

Read Arnold's first draft below and consider the following questions:

- **Does he explain clearly the purpose of his research?**

- **Does he explain clearly his method?**

- **Looking carefully at the context in which these words are used, what do you understand Arnold to mean by a) policy archeology; b) discourse; and c) rhetoric?**

- **What are the grounds for his claim that his methods have 'a high level of reliability and validity'?**

Parity: a new initiative or the same old story? A text-based research project (Draft)

Introduction

The need to establish equal status for vocational qualifications with general or 'academic' qualifications seems to be generally agreed. Recently, this issue has been in the news again, with cabinet ministers speaking of the need for a change of attitude towards vocational qualifications, and suggesting that the introduction of a vocational baccalaureate will be the best way to bring this about. However, there has been a history of similar claims made for qualifications such as the NVQ, the GNVQ, Foundations degrees, and various incarnations of the Apprenticeship. The purpose of this research report is to present, through a process of policy archeology, an analytical account of when and how these claims to parity have been made and to identify, if possible, the reasons why each, in its turn, met with failure.

Method

The method I chose to use was a textual analysis of White Papers published during the past 25 years and relating to vocational education. Most of these I was able to access in full text versions online. I also found hard copies of some of the earlier ones, published by Her Majesty's Stationery Office (HMSO) stored in the college library. I searched each document for three key words: 'parity'; 'esteem'; and 'status'. This enabled me to identify the political discourse about the relative status of vocational and general or 'academic' qualifications and to trace that discourse over the years in order to see whether or how it developed. I also used Wordle as a tool to analyse the frequency of key words in some of the more recent White Papers in order to discover the frequency with which 'parity' and the related vocabulary occurred. The data collected by these methods has a high level of reliability and validity.

Findings *I've still got to finish this section. This is just a very rough outline. Arnold*
It is possible to find claims of parity being made as early as the Education Act of 1944, in which the education provided by the newly established secondary modern schools was promised to have parity of esteem with that offered by grammar schools. This clearly didn't happen.

More recently, the 1991 White Paper, *Education and Training for the 21st Century*, which introduced, among other things, AS levels, vocational education in schools, and GNVQS, claimed that the government: 'want equal esteem' for vocational qualifications; and that these 'deserve equal recognition' (para 3.1). But these statements are not developed to explain how this might be achieved or what obstacles to equality need to be overcome. This isn't an argument, therefore, but appears to be simply rhetoric, using repetition about what <u>ought</u> to happen without actually engaging with the issue of what the government will <u>do</u> about it. Other documents I'm looking at include:

- *14–19 Education and Skills* (DfES, 2005) where the very title could be taken to suggest a distinction between education and training. 'Maths' 'English' and 'GCSE' show up large in Wordle, but 'vocational' not visible.
- *Further Education: Raising Skills, Improving Life Chances* (DfES, 2006)
- *Government Response to the Wolf Review of Vocational Education* (DfE, 2012).

Can you suggest any others I should use? I don't want this to get too big to manage in the time. Arnold.

Before we discuss the answers to the questions set out above, let's have a look first at Arnold's feedback from his tutor.

Tutor feedback

Arnold, you've made a great start. This is shaping up to be a very interesting assignment. Before you take it any further I'd like you to have a look at one or two points and keep them in mind while you're writing.

- First of all, you need to avoid making generalised statements unless you can follow them with a reference to something or someone that backs them up with evidence. For example, near the beginning you say: *'The need to establish equal status for vocational qualifications with general or "academic" qualifications seems to be generally agreed.'* What is your evidence for this? How can the reader be sure that you haven't simply pulled this assumption out of the air?
- On a related point, if you cite something someone has written or said, you must provide name, date and – if appropriate – publisher. So, for example, when you write that a Minister has been 'suggesting that the introduction of a vocational baccalaureate will be the best way to bring this about' you need to give details. Which minister? On what date? In what context? For example, if this was something you heard on a radio interview it might be '(Gove, 2013)'. In the reference list at the end it would give the full date of the broadcast and the name of the programme and radio channel. For example, 'Gove, M. (2013) Interview on *Today Programme*, BBC Radio 4, 12.05.13.' Providing these details allows your reader to check out what you've said and to pursue the research further if they wish. We sometimes refer to this safeguarding of our argument, this use of precise references bracketed within the text to protect each claim we make, as 'sandbagging'. So you should also think about sandbagging your next point: *'there has been a history of similar claims'*. Here you'd need a longer 'sandbag', which might look like this: '(for example, DES, 1991; DfES, 2005; DfES 2006)'.
- Try to avoid very short paragraphs as far as possible. They suggest that you're not developing your argument fully. For example, the first paragraph under 'Findings' doesn't explain <u>why</u> this is relevant to the status of vocational education.
- You need to develop your section on 'Method'. Although you explain what you're doing, you haven't demonstrated that you've read around the method you've used. There needs to be some reference to texts on research methods here to show that you've made <u>informed</u> choices about how to collect your data. This is what we mean by 'methodology'.

- You make a claim about validity and reliability, but it's not enough just to say this. You need to explain <u>why</u> you are able to make this claim. What is it about your method that will ensure the validity and reliability of the data? I could argue, playing devil's advocate, that you might see in the White Papers only what you're looking for. In other words, there could be researcher bias and subjectivity built into your approach. How would you counter that argument?
- As for choice about documents, the 1944 Act is well outside your time frame of 25 years. You need to <u>make a clear case for including it</u> here (and yes, I agree, there is a good case). Similarly, the first White Paper you analyse is from quite a while ago. You need to explain why you started with this one. Again, I can see why it was a good place to start – but you do need to explain this carefully. It's very important to give a clear rationale for all decisions made in the carrying out of your research.
- You make an excellent point when you distinguish between reasoned argument and simple rhetoric. Will you be making a similar textual analysis of the other key White Papers? If you're going to be drawing attention to rhetoric, you might want to read up about discourse analysis and see whether this is an approach you might want to use here.
- Finally, you need to be careful when writing up your research that you don't turn it into a <u>polemic</u>. A polemic is one-sided, written to persuade others to your point of view, and uses devices such as repetition or emotional language rather than reasoned argument. There's always a risk of lapsing into polemic when you hold strong views about what you are researching, and want to convince readers to agree with you. In fact, very clear examples of polemical writing can often be found in White Papers. As documents for promoting government policy, their main purpose is to persuade. So you might want to incorporate this point into your analysis, while avoiding using polemic yourself!

Come and see me if you'd like to discuss any of these points further.

CLOSE FOCUS CLOSE FOCUS CLOSE FOCUS CLOSE FOCUS

Arnold's tutor agrees that the 1944 Education Act and the 1991 White Paper were useful points of reference in the assignment, but he wants Arnold to explain *why*. How would you make the case for including them?

Discussion

Let's turn now to the questions you were asked to consider when reading Arnold's draft.

1. *Does he explain clearly the purpose of his research?* Yes, he does, although he is rather vague, as his tutor points out, about who has said what, and when. It is very important, when justifying your choice of research question, to demonstrate that you have a clear grasp of the background. The use of generalised statements suggests a lack of attention to detail and the inability to present a cogent argument.
2. *Does he explain clearly his method?* He tells us in general terms what he is going to do, but there are two key things missing here. He doesn't set out his argument *justifying* his use of this method. So he tells us what he has done, but not why. You'll remember from Chapter 1 that we refer to the *what* or *how* as the *method,* and the *why* as the *methodology.* The *methodology* is the philosophical justification and evaluation of the chosen method. It discusses how reliable and valid the data produced is likely to be, and why. It explores *epistemological* questions such as: *why*

or to what extent do I take the data gathered in this way to be a meaningful basis for constructing knowledge? As the tutor points out, Arnold needs to move beyond description of method and unsubstantiated claims about reliability, and begin to construct an argument to justify his choice, underpinned by references to relevant texts. These texts might consist of books about research method, such as this one; or they might be published research papers in which a similar methodology is discussed; or – best of all – both. As it stands, his paper offers no grounds for his claim that his methods have 'a high level of reliability and validity'.

3. *Looking carefully at the context in which these words are used, what do you understand Arnold to mean by: a) policy archeology; b) discourse; and c) rhetoric?* Policy archeology, as the name suggests, involves digging back through the documentary record to examine how policy has developed, changed, or repeated itself. It is a process which enables the researcher to identify recurring themes, contradictions, and changes in underlying assumptions and values. When Arnold excavates back to 1944 in his search for the origins of terminology such as 'parity', he is engaging in a form of *policy archeology*, a methodological approach usually attributed to Scheurich (1994). A discussion of those other terms, *discourse* and *rhetoric*, can be found in the section below.

Ideology, discourse, rhetoric and polemic

To explore these terms we need to begin with another one: *Ideology*. An ideology is a belief, point of view, or set of values which is held unquestioningly and uncritically. We encounter this word most commonly in the contexts of politics and religion: the communist regimes of the twentieth century, for example; or the fundamentalist beliefs of America's 'Christian' far right. These ideologies, because they do not acknowledge the possibility of debate or contradiction, render alternatives invisible. An ideology that forbids education for girls, once it is entrenched, makes what we would see as an injustice something that is perfectly acceptable and 'normal'. The injustice of it becomes invisible. Similarly, an ideology based on the necessity of privilege, for example, would take it for granted – take it as common sense, in fact – that it is acceptable for wealthy parents to buy educational advantage for their children. The ideology that has had the greatest impact on UK education and training in the past three or four decades is a belief that introducing market forces into educational provision will improve the quality of teaching and learning. Competition between colleges and between schools has become the accepted norm, to the extent that we can forget there are alternatives – such as the collaborative strategic planning that used to be co-ordinated by local authorities. And this taking for granted of the 'naturalness' of operating a market in such a context (with the implication that education or training is a commodity rather than a right or a good in itself) illustrates perfectly how ideologies work, persuading us to take a set of values and beliefs as the only one it is possible to hold.

Most government policy documents, such as White Papers, are expressions of a set of political beliefs and values – an ideology. And the way in which that ideology is expressed is one of the meanings of *discourse*. A *discourse* is the expression, open or covert, of a point of view or belief system which is presented to be taken for granted and not questioned. Unlike an argument, a discourse doesn't necessarily depend on clear reasoning supported by evidence. In fact it will often use a very careful selection of 'facts', omitting any that don't fit with its point of view, presenting only a partial picture masquerading as the whole truth. It may also make use of emotional or stirring language to hide the fact that it offers no evidence to support its argument. This reliance on carefully chosen words which add persuasiveness to a discourse is known as *rhetoric*. All of these elements of discourse are easily found in White Papers, and also sometimes in documents designed to promote an institution, such as mission statements. Finding evidence of such discourses and using these to identify the underlying ideology is often referred to as *discourse analysis*. It is this approach that Arnold's tutor, in his feedback, is suggesting he might adopt.

The other term that Arnold's tutor introduces is polemic, and he explains it clearly as an 'argument' which doesn't acknowledge, or simply dismisses, the possibility of a counter-argument. It is something we should carefully avoid in our academic writing, and be watchful for in the writing of others.

CLOSE FOCUS CLOSE FOCUS CLOSE FOCUS CLOSE FOCUS **CLOSE FOCUS**

Arnold's tutor advises him to 'sandbag' all unsubstantiated or general statements with clear references. Read through Arnold's piece again and identify a) where these are needed; b) what information he needs in order to do this; and c) how he will set these references out. (The tutor provides guidance and templates for this in the second point on his written feedback.)

Research using college documents

We've looked at some ways we might analyse national policy documents. Another approach, of course, would be to evaluate how far the claims made in such documents about the efficacy or likely impact of new government policy initiatives prove to be the case when the policy is put into practice within your college. Or you might want to look at the extent to which internal policy documents, such as policies to support inclusion or set out acceptable codes of behaviour, accurately reflect current relevant legislation.

Arnold, still interested in the concept of 'parity', decides to have a close look at his college's policy on Inclusion, as this is where issues such as equality will be defined and applied to the college context. On carrying out a textual analysis of the policy, he finds that the word 'parity' is not used at all. When he copies the full text into Wordle he is able to identify *participate, equality, potential* and, of course, *inclusion* as the key recurrent words. He then carries out a content analysis and comparison. This involves him reading the policy carefully and comparing its coverage and content with the inclusion policies of two other colleges in the same region.

TASK TASK TASK TASK **TASK** TASK TASK **TASK** TASK

Below is an extract from Arnold's draft of his findings. Read it carefully and make a note of any comments or questions you have.

Analysis of Z College Inclusion Policy
Draft findings
My main concern, after an initial reading, was the lack of clarity about what the processes are in case a breach of the policy needs to be reported; and who should be involved at each stage. Section 4, headed 'Responsibilities', sets out who is responsible for what. For example:
   'Members of staff are responsible for supporting the aims of this policy,
   promoting equal opportunity, and contributing to an inclusive environment.'
   (College Z Inclusion Policy, p.5, paragraph 4.6)

The difficulty here is that, not only is there no guidance as to what it might look like when these responsibilities are being carried out in practice, but also there is no indication of the line of communication staff should follow if an incident needs to be reported. This lack of clarity may make the effective implementation of the policy more difficult than it needs to be. This problem is also evident in a later paragraph headed 'Breach of Policy':

'The college encourages informal resolution of issues relevant to this policy.'

(College Z Inclusion Policy, p.6, paragraph 7.1)

This could be taken to mean that staff and complainants are expected to resolve such issues unsupported. It is evident from the Inclusion Policies of other colleges (for example, College X and College Y) that other institutions offer support for staff. For example, College X's policy states:

'The College provides advisors and mediators to support staff and students in resolving issues of non-adherence.' (College X Inclusion Policy, p.3, paragraph 6)

I am aware, from my professional experience, that my own college, College Z, also does provide such support, in fact; but fails to make this apparent in the wording of the policy, as we have seen.

Discussion

Arnold is doing something very useful here. He is evaluating his institution's Inclusion Policy not only by a close textual analysis, but also by comparison with policies drawn up by similar institutions. Again this is 'desktop' research, in that it doesn't involve participants. But the usual conventions of academic writing still apply when he comes to write this up. You'll see, for example, that he has:

i) *Presented quotes correctly in a way that distinguishes them clearly from his own work.* He's done this by using italics and quotation marks, and insetting them in a paragraph of their own.

ii) *References all quotes fully*. These are not drawn from published documents such as books or journals; but nevertheless he knows that he must cite their source clearly, so that anyone reading his research report can access the full document and check that the material he has quoted is a) accurate and b) has not been taken out of context. He gives the page number *and* the paragraph number, which it is possible to do in this case because the format of internal policy documents normally uses numbered paragraphing, as does that of government documents such as White Papers. Citing the paragraph can be particularly useful if you have access a document online on which page numbers do not appear.

iii) *Maintained the anonymity of the colleges whose policies he is discussing*. This demonstrates that he is applying research ethics. He has decided to refer to the colleges by letters of the alphabet. He could, as an alternative, have referred to them by allocating numbers. Or he could have given them fictional names, such as Primrose College, Bluebell College and so on. Fictional names have the advantage that they can infuse liveliness into a research report. On the other hand, there is a potential disadvantage in that they may inadvertently convey some degree of researcher bias through the choice of names. I've seen an example of this where the researcher decided to name institutions after Dickens' characters. 'Pickwick College' and 'Copperfield College' were no problem; 'Scrooge College' on the other hand, was a rather unfortunate choice.

However, perhaps you noticed that Arnold doesn't explain to us how he selected the material he chose to quote. He needs to reassure us, as readers of his research, that he isn't approaching this research with the intention simply of finding something to criticise, but with an open mind and in a spirit of exploration to see what is there and whether it works. To do this he needs to tell us what criteria he's used for selection. He could say, for example, that he has chosen extracts which are representative, or illustrative, of the policy as a whole or of a particular section of it. He also needs to point out the strengths of the policy, if there are any. If he doesn't, he risks his report appearing to be a polemic or flawed by researcher bias.

A SUMMARY OF **KEY POINTS**

In this chapter we have discussed:
> **the difference between participant-centred and 'desktop' research;**
> **ways of analysing documents such as White Papers and college policy documents;**
> **the importance of avoiding generalised statements, and the need to safeguard our argument by the use of precise references bracketed within the text;**
> **the importance of distinguishing between reasoned argument and simple rhetoric in our own work and the work of others;**
> **the importance of recognising polemic in the work of others, and avoiding it in our own;**
> **how to use *discourse analysis* in order to identify the underlying ideology of any of the documents we are researching.**

We have also identified some useful terms to use when writing about documentary research. These include: *desktop research; policy archeology; policy analysis; discourse; discourse analysis; polemic; ideology.*

Branching options

You may like to choose one of the following activities which are designed to help you apply what you've learnt from this chapter to your own practice. The first encourages you, as a professional, to develop your skills of reflection; the second asks you to take an evaluative approach consistent with an initial teaching qualification in the sector; and the third is designed to support skills of critical analysis appropriate to post-qualification CPD or Masters level study.

Reflection

Choose either a recent White Paper relevant to FE and vocational training, or a policy document from your own college, and use Wordle to identify its most frequently used words. What insights, if any, does this give you into the dominant discourse of your chosen document?

Evaluation

Select a recent White Paper relating to Further Education and vocational training:

1. How would you summarise the discourse in this document? What does this tell you about the ideology which underlies it?
2. Identify at least three sentences or paragraphs which provide examples of: a) rhetoric; and b) polemic.

Critical analysis

Look again at Arnold's work on the White Papers and re-write his method and methodology section for him, drawing on the feedback from his tutor and on what you have learnt from this chapter about textual and discourse analysis.

REFERENCES AND FURTHER READING REFERENCES AND FURTHER READING

A methodological argument for the use of policy archeology can be found in:

Scheurich, J. J. (1994) Policy Archeology: a new policy studies methodology. *Journal of Education Policy,* 9 (4): 296–316.

Important: Notice that it is *the title of the journal*, and not the title of the paper which is emphasised in this reference. This is an important point to remember when setting out references to papers in academic journals, and one which many people slip up on. The same rule applies when you make reference to a specific chapter in an edited book. It is the title of the book, not the title of the chapter, which is emphasised. If you look carefully through the reference lists at the end of books or research papers you will see this rule being applied.

Other texts you might find useful are:

Atkins, L. and Wallace, S. (2012) *Qualitative Research in Education*. London: Sage. (Chapter 9)

Ozga, J. (1999) *Policy Research in Educational Settings*. Oxford: Oxford University Press.

9
What does it all mean? Analysing your findings

The objectives of this chapter

This chapter offers advice on how to make sense of the information or data collected. How do we 'analyse' an interview, for example? What are we to make of our observation findings? As well as practical advice about the interrogation, analysis, selection and presentation of data, the chapter looks at the theoretical and philosophical questions which are raised by the researcher's decisions about what is to be offered in evidence and what is not.

The chapter will introduce and discuss some useful terminology, including: *evidence interrogation; representative; illustrative; indicative; categorisation; theme; synthesis; truth; proof; material evidence; verbatim; archive.*

Introduction

Analysing our findings is one of the most exciting parts of the research process; and also perhaps the most dangerous. It involves the use of concepts and terminology which are more slippery than they seem and which need to be handled critically and with care. Words such as *evidence* and *proof* and *truth* can lure us into making claims which are untenable, both factually and philosophically. Therefore, if we are wise, we will approach this stage of our research initially as a philosopher might, by asking ourselves, *'How, and to what extent, do the data that I've gathered enable me to know something that I didn't know before?'* This, as you will remember from earlier chapters, is a question about epistemology – about what it means to *know* something.

What is truth?

For example, when we say that something is 'true', what assumptions are we making about the level of *proof* this implies? You are perhaps familiar with the logical equation which tells us that if $A=B$ and $B=C$, then obviously we can safely assume that A must equal C. But if we were to express this in another form, such as: 'Men walk on two legs and Sister Brenda walks on two legs, and so we can safely assume that Sister Brenda is a man', we can see how this sort of 'logical' reasoning about our data can lead us up the garden path, where ostriches and performing elephants end up in the same category as the Archbishop of Canterbury. What's more, even our initial statement cannot be presented as a general truth, since it is sadly not the case that all men are able to walk on two legs. In carrying out and presenting our analysis of the data we've gathered, we must be meticulous in our reasoning and the way in which we word our findings.

Can we trust the evidence?

While *truth* and *proof* may be problematical concepts, we could be forgiven for assuming that there is a straightforward and common understanding of what we mean by *evidence*. But even here we must take a cautious and critical approach. One of the most famous English philosophers, Jeremy Bentham (1748–1831) wrote, in *A Treatise on Judicial Evidence* (1825), that legal testimony, or evidence, must be substantiated – that is, backed up – by material proof such as objects or other visual phenomena. His argument was that objects, things, evidence that we can see and touch, are trustworthy (in his words, 'incorruptible') and not subject to distortions of opinion, bias and human error, as spoken testimony may be. Now, for us, as educational researchers, this is quite a troubling claim and one that we need to think through carefully. The vast majority of small-scale educational practitioner research is qualitative rather than quantitative. That is, it uses as its data what people do or say, rather than measurements and statistics. And there are two very good practical reasons for this. First, education is a lived experience, complex and nuanced, which is not meaningfully reduceable to numbers – for teachers, if not politicians. Second, numerical data only become convincing when you are working with very large numbers – and working with very large numbers requires substantial time and resourcing which most teacher-researchers simply do not have. So, when we are analysing interview recordings or questionnaires or our observations of classroom interactions, in Bentham's terms we are choosing to deal with evidence which is corruptible or subject to distortion, and we need to be aware of this and take all possible measures to minimise the possibility of researcher bias.

But, now that we've got our critical hat on, we're not going to let Bentham off the hook so easily. He tells us that 'material proof' – what we can see and measure – is not vulnerable to bias or error as human testimony is; but we can challenge this assertion. Imagine, for example, that you live alone and, returning home in the snow, find a set of large footprints leading up to your front door. Someone has entered your house! You run around to the back. No footprints anywhere. Whoever went in by the front door must still be in there! The footprints are material proof. You can see them; you can measure them. You can photograph them with your phone. They lead up to the door and there are none leading away. So you call the police. While you're waiting for them to arrive you go around to your neighbour's house. She's on the phone complaining to the Post Office. The postman – a bit of a joker – has been amusing himself everywhere he's delivered mail by walking away backwards in his own footprints.

Material evidence *can* be misread. We must still work out what it *means*; and this is the case whether we are talking about murder weapons or statistics. The potential for error and bias is always there in the very process of interpretation.

TASK TASK **TASK** TASK **TASK** TASK **TASK** TASK **TASK** TASK

We're going to look now at how one teacher tries to bear all of this in mind as she undertakes the analysis of the data she has collected. Stella has used a case study approach to investigate the impact of teaching styles on learner motivation within her department. This means that she has interviews, questionnaires and observations to analyse. Read the extract below from the first draft of her research assignment, in which she explains how she has approached the analysis, and consider the following questions:

- **Why do you think Stella has 'archived' the interview recordings?**
- **What does Stella mean by 'verbatim'?**

- In your own words, what strategy does Stella use to minimise the risk of bias in her choice of what quotes to present from the interviews?
- What do you think she means by 'key words'?
- Why, according to her, does she analyse the observation data last?

Stella. First draft.

How I analysed the data

The first set of data I analysed were the three interviews with colleagues. The assignment deadline meant that I did not have time to make complete transcripts of each interview, so I used the recordings as the basis for my analysis. These recordings are now archived safely in order to maintain confidentiality (BERA, 2011). The only passages I transcribed verbatim were those I wished to present as quotes in my findings. The basis on which I selected these particular passages was that they were typical or representative of the interview findings, or illustrative of a particular theme in the relevant literature. I am aware that selecting particular passages to transcribe and quote leaves me vulnerable to accusations of researcher bias on the grounds that I could just be choosing to quote extracts which support my own views or argument. Being aware of this, I have justified the inclusion of each quote as it appears, explaining my purpose in selecting it. I analysed the interview responses by identifying any common themes and using these as categories for the analysis. I also looked for the recurrence of any key words. I did this by listening to each recording several times. If I had had time to transcribe each interview fully I could have used technological means such as Wordle for this purpose. I then looked to see whether and how the key words fitted with the themes or categories I'd identified. This systematic approach minimised the possibility of researcher bias by making it less likely that I would simply see in the data what I wanted or expected to see.

I used a similar approach on the responses to the open questions on the questionnaire, categorising them and identifying any recurring words. Here I was able to use Wordle. The responses to the closed questions were simply to provide me with demographic data. I used this to look for correlations between, for example, age or length of teaching experience and strategies for classroom behaviour management. The classroom observations were the most problematical source of data in terms of guarding against bias. I had chosen not to make video recordings, as these might have disrupted normal activity. My data was therefore in the form of my own observation notes, and it is possible that I may have applied my own agenda in choosing what and what not to note down. Therefore in carrying out my analysis I tried to minimise possible bias in two ways. Firstly, I analysed the observations only after I had analysed the other data so that any researcher bias in them would not lead me to look for corroboration in the interviews and questionnaires. Secondly, I used the categories and recurring words found in the other data as a starting point for analysing the observations. I cannot claim that my analysis of data overall was not subjective, but my approach was at least designed to minimise researcher bias as far as possible.

Discussion

Before we consider the answers to the questions listed above, let's just look at this extract from Stella's draft as a whole. Her purpose in writing this section is not to describe and discuss what she found – she'll do that later in her assignment – but to explain the procedures she used to extract those findings from the data. Her concern is to anticipate and pre-empt any criticism of her findings on the grounds of them being contaminated by the leaking of her own assumptions and prejudices into the analytical process. This step-by-step explanation of how she approached this crucial stage of her research serves to strengthen her argument that the evidence she'll be presenting can be accepted as reliable. When you write up your own research project it's important to keep this in mind. It's easy to remember to include your literature review, your method and methodology and your findings; but it's surprising how many practitioner researchers forget to explain the details of the analytical processes they have used to arrive at those findings.

So, getting back to our questions, why has Stella 'archived' the interview recordings? The answer here is that, lacking a written transcript, she realises she will still need to be able to point to 'material evidence' to support her findings. In the case of a CPD coursework assignment, she would be wise to retain this archive until her mark or award is confirmed by the exam board. If she aims to publish her research she will need to keep the archive for longer. Because she will have promised her participants confidentiality in line with BERA guidelines, the archived recording will need to be somewhere secure, such as a password protected file.

What does Stella mean by 'verbatim'? This is a term from the Latin meaning 'word for word'. A verbatim transcription is one which sets out *exactly what was said*, without any paraphrasing or omissions. The full Latin phrase is *verbatim et literatim* – 'word for word and letter for letter'. However, we must remember that capturing the exact words that someone has said is rather like displaying one of Bentham's objects as material proof. They are still open to interpretation and the imposition of various meanings, not least since elements such as intonation and facial expression are stripped away in the transfer from spoken interview to written word.

Stella goes into some detail about her selection of quotes for presentation, and it's important that we understand what she's saying here. She acknowledges that there is always a risk that the qualitative researcher may be accused of biased selectivity when choosing a few brief quotes from the thousands of words in a participant's response. How can we, as readers, know that she isn't cherry picking just those utterances that are in agreement with her own views or which support her own premeditated argument? To avoid this uncertainty she lays her cards on the table and tells us exactly what criteria she has used for her choice. These are that the quotes should be typical of the majority of responses to that question, representative of a particular emerging theme in the interviews as a whole, or illustrative of a key point in the assignment; for example, one emerging from the relevant literature. Similarly, when she uses the term 'key words', she is referring to ideas or terminology which recur repeatedly across the interview or questionnaire responses. This recurrence can be taken as an indication of the reliability of the data.

And why does she analyse the observation data last? Her argument here is that these observation data are, of all three sets, the most vulnerable to researcher bias. They consist of *her* notes and *her* memories from the observations *she* has carried out. In Bentham's terms it is entirely untrustworthy. And Stella is perfectly aware that there is indeed a lot of room here for subjectivity. If she began her analysis with this data it might generate skewed categories or themes which could then contaminate the findings from the interviews and the questionnaires. The decision to deal with it last makes good sense.

CLOSE FOCUS CLOSE FOCUS CLOSE FOCUS CLOSE FOCUS CLOSE FOCUS

So far in this chapter we talked a great deal about *data* and *evidence*. Do you think there is a distinction between the two; and if so, how would you describe the difference?

TASK TASK TASK TASK TASK TASK TASK TASK TASK TASK

Having explained her approach to analysing the data, Stella now has to write up her findings. But before we read that section of her assignment, let's have a look at the interview data she's been working on. Unlike Stella, we've had time to make a complete transcript of the three short interviews. Your task now is to read through these and follow Stella's example by identifying any common themes or categories and looking for extracts to quote which will illustrate these. You'll then have an opportunity to compare your own findings with Stella's.

Interview 1: 'Zara'

S: So thanks for agreeing to be interviewed and can you tell me a bit about your own approach to motivation and behaviour management in the classroom?

Z: You're welcome. Well, I suppose a lot of what you'd call behaviour management comes directly from thinking on my feet. I mean, you can't really plan for it, can you? Not unless you know you've got someone in the group who always plays up or causes trouble. If that's the case, I just make sure I've got a lesson plan that keeps that particular culprit so occupied that he or she forgets to play up.

S: How do you mean? Can you say a bit more about that?

Z: Well, like I'll organise activities that give the troublemaker a role where they're always busy and getting lots of attention so they don't need to get attention by playing up. Like, if it was a group discussion I'd get X [a notoriously disruptive student] to be the observer who has to make sure everyone's had a say and then feed back to the class. Or if I was presenting stuff via PowerPoint I'd get him to work the remote and...

S: That sounds a bit risky!

Z: It's weird, isn't it? I give him stuff like that to do and he loves it. He knows if he messes up he won't get the chance to show off again.

S: But you have to be quite confident to take that sort of approach, don't you? I mean, I can't imagine a trainee teacher...

Z: No, well, I suppose a lot of it comes down to knowing the learners, doesn't it? Knowing how far you can trust them. And them knowing you, and knowing how far they can push you. I mean with me they know: it's this far and no further. But they can't get to know you unless you're confident enough to be yourself with them. And you know what I thinks a problem?

S: Go on.

Z: What I thinks a problem is that new trainees are being forced to do all this whizzy technology and it just gets between them and the learners. They should be learning how to build a relationship, and instead they're learning how to tweet and blog and – basically – how to keep the poor bloody learners at arm's length.

S: You sound like a grumpy old woman.

Z: I know! And I'm only 29!

S: So if I asked you whether you think teaching style has an impact on learner motivation in FE...

Z: Oh yes. Completely. It so does.

Interview 2: 'Desmond'

S: Thanks for agreeing to be interviewed. Can we start by you telling me a bit about how you see motivation and behaviour management in the context of your own teaching?

D: What? Whose motivation? Mine or theirs? [Laughter] Yeah, well I don't have too much trouble with that, really.

S: But when you do have trouble with learners' motivation or behaviour, what do you do?

D: Shout at them? [Laughs] No, seriously. What do I do? I suppose I try to explain that it's only them who have something to lose. That they're only doing damage to themselves. You know?

S: But they're not, are they? Only doing it to themselves, I mean? They're spoiling...

D: They're spoiling the experience for everyone else. Yeah. Yeah, they are. But, you know, telling them that just doesn't work – not in my experience, anyway. The best thing, the best thing to get them back on task is to inject a change of direction, a change of activity, maybe. Do something a bit more exciting. Trouble is, you can't be exciting all the time. There's stuff you have to do and stuff they have to learn. And some learning demands hard work and concentration, you know? You can't dumb it all down and jazz it all up just so no one acts difficult. If they're here to learn, they're here to learn. Not to be entertained or bribed or patronised just so they'll behave and give us an easy time. No.

S: So do you think teaching style has an impact on learner motivation in FE?

D: Yes. Oh yes, absolutely. But I don't think you can solve everything or get every learner on board just by virtue of your teaching style. There's a whole political and social set of factors that are causing kids to disengage from learning, and we can't even begin to address those from the classroom end.

Interview 3: 'Jude'

S: Okay. So thanks for agreeing to be interviewed today. And could you tell me a bit about your thoughts on motivation and behaviour management in the classroom?

J: Yeah. Happy to do it. I mean, what I think is that you've either got it or you haven't. Know what I mean?

S: Not really. Could you...?

J: I mean it's not something you can teach people. It's sort of part of your personality or it's not. It's like charisma, you know? It sort of comes naturally. It's part of who you are. So you can be in this business 20 years but if you haven't got it you'll never learn it. You get me?

S: So you don't think it can be developed as part of CPD or through experience; you know, trial and error?

J: Nope. I mean, you've only got to look around, yeah?

S: But if it's only to do with personality, are you saying that learners' motivation is entirely dependent on who's teaching them.

J: Right.

S: And that in your view it's nothing to do with *how* they teach, but simply the teacher's personality?

J: Right.

S: But hang on. Doesn't the teacher's personality to some extent determine how they teach? So a more confident teacher will try more high risk, interesting methods for example?

J: Chicken and egg, man. Chicken and egg.

S: So you don't think that it's possible, through CPD, to develop and extend teachers' repertoire of teaching styles and methods so that they're better able to motivate and engage learners?

J: Nope. Either they've got it or they haven't.

> **S:** Right. So let me ask you, finally: Do you think, on the whole, that teaching style has an impact on learner motivation in FE?
>
> **J:** Yeah, man. But, like I say, you're born with it, get me?

Take some time now to analyse these three interview transcripts. Keeping Stella's research question always in mind, see whether you can identify:

- **themes or categories that are common to all three;**
- **extracts you could quote which would illustrate these themes or categories.**

When you have completed this task, compare your analysis to Stella's, which you will find below.

> **Stella. Draft analysis of interviews 1–3.**
> In terms of the key research question, all three interviewees expressed the view that teaching style has an impact on learners' motivation in FE. Moreover, all three interviewees intimated that they themselves were able to motivate their learners and manage learner behaviour successfully through their ability to adopt appropriate methods and styles of teaching. A number of further themes emerged from the interviews, which I have categorised as: a) the role of experience; b) the causes of disengagement; and c) the key to engaging learners. There was no unanimous agreement on these, each interviewee expressing an individual view. These themes are discussed below. The extracts quoted from each interview are selected as illustrative of the point each interviewee is making.
>
> *a) The role of experience*
> Two interviewees (Z and D) expressed the view that teachers learn through experience the effectiveness of certain teaching styles for engaging learner interest. For example, D explains that: *'Telling them that [they're spoiling things for others] just doesn't work – not in my experience, anyway'.* And Z points out that such skills grow with practice: *'you have to be quite confident to take that sort of approach, don't you? I mean, I can't imagine a trainee teacher'.* J, on the other hand, suggested that experience alone counted for nothing, and that the ability to motivate and engage learners is: *'part of who you are. So you can be in this business 20 years but if you haven't got it you'll never learn it'.*
>
> *b) Causes of disengagement*
> Each of the three interviewees suggested a different cause for learners' lack of motivation. In D's view the underlying causes of learner disengagement are social and political, and that therefore the ability of even the most experienced teachers to solve the problem is limited: *'There's a whole political and social set of factors that are causing kids to disengage from learning, and we can't even begin to address those from the classroom end'.* Z, on the other hand, was of the opinion that the teacher-learner relationship is crucial to ensuring learner engagement, and that current trends towards regarding technology as a teaching method rather than simply as a resource are ultimately counter-productive: *'all this whizzy technology and it just gets between them and the learners'.* J, however, attributed it to the teacher's personality.
>
> *c) The key to engaging learners*
> Each of the three interviewees offered a different view of the key factor necessary for ensuring learner engagement. In Z's view, motivation depended on the teacher getting to know the learners as individuals: *'a lot of it comes down to knowing the learners';* while for D it was

crucial to be willing and able to introduce: *'a change of activity, maybe. Do something a bit more exciting'.* J, however, maintained that the only relevant factor was the personality of the teacher, and suggested that: *'you've either got it or you haven't'.*

Discussion

How did your own analysis compare with Stella's? Notice how she has constructed it. We can use her analysis to begin a useful template, which would look like this:

Template	Stella's analysis
1. What is the overall response to the research question?	*All interviewees agree that teaching style has an impact on learners' motivation in FE.*
2. What response[s] do the interviewees have in common?	*All able to motivate and manage learner behaviour by adopting appropriate methods and styles of teaching.*
3. A summary of further themes.	*a) the role of experience; b) the causes of disengagement; and c) the key to engaging learners.*
4. Discuss each theme in detail, using quotes from the interviewee to illustrate key points.	e.g.: *Two interviewees (Z and D) expressed the view that teachers learn the effectiveness of this through experience. For example, D explains that: 'Telling them that [they're spoiling things for others] just doesn't work – not in my experience, anyway'.*
5. Link each of these themes to the relevant literature that you have discussed.	
6. Summarise the findings, with reference to your research question. What have you discovered?	

You'll see that in her draft as it appears here, Stella has not yet completed stages 5 and 6 of her analysis, perhaps because she has still to analyse the questionnaire responses and the classroom observations before she can summarise this section of her work. But what she has produced so far is helpful to us in demonstrating how themes can be identified, summarised and illustrated with quoted material. She explains clearly how and why the quoted material has been selected, and makes sure it is clearly distinct from her own writing by italicising it, as well as using speech marks or quotation marks to show that she is quoting verbatim. If these quotes had been a little longer she might have chosen to inset them as well; but these are brief enough to present within the existing paragraph. Her analysis identifies for us both the common ground shared by the interviewees, as well as each one's very different agenda. If we take this draft together with her account, earlier in this chapter, of how she approached the data analysis, we can begin to see how this section of her research paper is taking shape.

CLOSE FOCUS CLOSE FOCUS **CLOSE FOCUS** CLOSE FOCUS **CLOSE FOCUS**

Have a look again at Stella's third interview, the one with Jude. What do you notice about Stella's interview technique here? How would you evaluate it? You might find it useful to refer back to Chapter 6 to help you to identify examples of closed questions and leading questions.

Presenting the data

We've seen how Stella has approached the presentation of her research data, and we can see that this activity falls into distinct stages.

1. First we scrutinise our data by reading it, listening to it, or watching it, depending on the form it takes.
2. Second, we think about it, we reflect and mull it over. We make sure we are noticing the overall 'shape' as well as the detail.
3. Third, we begin to identify key themes and ideas and select the quotes which we will present.
4. Fourth – and this is essential – we make sure that we can explain how and why we have identified these themes and made this selection; why and how these are relevant to our research question and are an accurate representation of the data overall.

We can apply a research vocabulary to this activity, as Wellington (2000) does, when he sets it out as a six-stage process consisting of: *Immersion, Reflection, Analysis, Synthesis; Location and Relation; and Selection and Presentation* (Wellington, 2000: 135). The term *synthesis* here means looking for common themes, arguments and ideas and summarising and expressing them in our own words – a process with which we've seen Stella engage. By *Location and Relation* Wellington means the process by which we relate these themes and ideas to existing literature and research, seeing how they 'fit'. Do they match what the literature has led us to expect? Do they seem to contradict it and show us something new? This is the stage of the analysis which Stella has not yet completed.

Data and evidence

Earlier in this chapter you were posed a question: Are data and evidence the same thing; and, if not, what is the distinction? One answer is that it is useful to see these two as quite distinct. *Data* is the word to describe all the information and observations and responses and conversations that you have gathered in the course of your research. The *evidence* is what you glean from all those data to arrive at your findings and to support your argument for those findings. In research we talk about raw data. Raw data doesn't propose or support an argument; it just is. The researcher looks at it and considers it, rather as a police officer might consider a crime scene. Gradually a picture emerges. Some of what she sees and hears will be incidental; some will be crucial evidence in supporting the argument she puts together to justify an arrest. Stella's interviews tell her a good deal about her interviewees. But she, as researcher, must decide what parts of these data are relevant to her research question and can be regarded as evidence; and which are equally interesting – such as Jude's verbal tics or Desmond's hard line on tolerance – but do not constitute useful evidence in reaching an answer to that question.

Working with numerical data

As discussed earlier, small-scale educational practitioner research tends to focus on qualitative data because of restrictions of scale and the nature of education as a lived experience. However, sometimes it is useful or appropriate to offer some measurement in support of our findings.

Let's say, for example, that Stella had decided to express some of her findings also in a quantitative form. It is unlikely that she would do so; but imagine for a moment that she wants to do this with her interview findings. She might say: *'100 per cent of those interviewed held the view that teaching style has an impact on learners' motivation in FE.'* This, of course, would be true, as would the statement, *'100 per cent of interviewees intimated that they themselves were able to motivate their learners and manage learner behaviour successfully through their ability to adopt appropriate methods and styles of teaching.'* However, we can see at once that this way of expressing her findings could be very misleading, because it gives the impression that large numbers – possibly in the hundreds – of interviewees were involved. Three teachers saying the same thing does not have the same impact or implications for reliability as a unanimous agreement of 300, say. Percentages used like this can cloud the findings and even mislead. What if Stella, using the same approach, had written, *'33.3 per cent of those interviewed maintained that the only relevant factor was the personality of the teacher'*? How could a reader know – as we happen to know – that 33.3 per cent of this sample represents just one interviewee? Whether results like this are presented as percentages or as pie charts or as block graphs, it is always important to *cite actual numbers* alongside whatever method of representation you are using. Failure to do so could be seen as potentially misleading.

A SUMMARY OF **KEY POINTS**

In this chapter we have discussed:
> the assumptions we make when we describe something as 'true';
> the idea that material proof is more reliable than human testimony; and the argument that actually both are vulnerable to bias or error;
> the distinction between data and evidence;
> procedures and stages in the analysis of data, including the identification of common themes which may be used as categories for the analysis; and the search for recurring words or phrases;
> the selection and presentation of quotes;
> approaches to the presentation of evidence;
> the caution necessary when presenting numerical data.

We have also identified some useful terms to use when writing about the analysis of our research data. These include: *evidence interrogation; representative; illustrative; indicative; categorisation; theme; synthesis; truth; proof; material evidence; verbatim; archive.*

Branching options

You may like to choose one of the following activities which are designed to help you apply what you've learnt from this chapter to your own practice. The first encourages you, as a professional, to develop your skills of reflection; the second asks you to take an evaluative approach consistent with an initial teaching qualification in the sector; and the third is designed to support skills of critical analysis appropriate to post-qualification CPD or Masters level study.

Reflection

Go back to Stella's first draft where she explains the analytical procedures she has followed. You'll perhaps have noticed that she hasn't made any references to research literature at any point to support her argument. If you were advising her, where would you suggest that these references or 'sandbags' are needed?

Evaluation

You'll have noticed from the transcripts that Stella doesn't ask her interview questions in exactly the same way to each participant.

1. Do you think this matters, for example, in terms of the reliability of the data they produce? Think this through carefully, and then set out an argument to support your answer.
2. In interview 3 (Jude) Stella seems to be falling into the trap of asking closed questions and talking more than the interviewee. How would you respond to each of Jude's replies in order to draw out lengthier and more complex answers that are relevant to the research question?

Critical analysis

You'll remember that Stella also has to analyse data from her questionnaires. Below you'll find eight responses to question 3 of that questionnaire. Using the data analysis approach that we have discussed in this chapter, carry out a category analysis, identifying themes and key words.

Question 3: Describe an instance of when you have successfully used a teaching style or method specifically in order to encourage disaffected learners to engage with their learning.

Responses

- *I have a level 2 group that aren't able to listen or concentrate to 'teacher talk'. So I made a video of myself delivering some crucial lesson content against different backgrounds, two minutes in a supermarket, two minutes at a skate park, two minutes on the bus, etc. I realise this is using video as a resource really and not a method but it did get them paying attention. I'm not sure how much of what I was saying actually went in though. And it's not something I can be doing all the time, obviously.*
- *My teaching style is energetic and enthusiastic. I don't 'use' it – it's just how I always teach. And that always keeps learners engaged and happy.*
- *Now and then I promise the workshop group a game if they pay attention and get on with their coursework. Games they like are quizzes in teams and simulations where they work in teams as well. Anything competitive. Can't do it often or it would lose novelty value. Is it a method? Do they learn anything? Not sure.*
- *I find the foundation degree students don't really like groupwork and they just switch off so I tend to give them lectures with the powerpoint and follow it with Q&A and that way they seem to feel we're making best use of time.*

- *They like doing a bake-off. If they get the kitchens cleaned up in good time three days in a row I organise a bake-off like on TV with me doing a commentary. Not always cakes though obviously.*
- *I plan all my lessons with changes of activity every 20 minutes so I don't have a problem with disengagement. Keeping up the pace and planning it properly always works for me. No particular example stands out.*
- *I had a very difficult group last year and I decided to try talking less and getting them to do more so instead of giving them information I suggested they find it out online and I would rank them in small groups according to their online research skills. This is an approach that's worked really well. I make sure they share around what they've researched, so the less skilled ones don't miss out and obviously I check the accuracy of what they've got. But it works and it's changed my whole approach to teaching really because I get much more time now to get to know them instead of just talking at them.*
- *I've found attitude and manner really help, if that's what's meant here by 'style'. Looking as though I'm enjoying teaching the subject and being with the learners has a visibly positive effect on their morale. If I just stood there looking fed up and as if I'd rather be somewhere else then they'd obviously not be motivated or engaged. That's much more significant than methods in my view. So I think you're asking the wrong question.*

REFERENCES AND FURTHER READING

This chapter, like the book as a whole, has focused on the collection and analysis of qualitative data. If you would like to find out more about how to analyse and present *quantitative* data, you will find this topic dealt with in:

Cohen, L., Manion, L. and Morrison, K. (2011) *Research Methods in Education* (7th edition). London: Routledge.

If you would like to see what more Wellington has to say about the analysis and presentation of data you can find details in:

Wellington, J. (2000) *Educational Research: Contemporary Issues and Practical Approaches*. London: Continuum.

10
Sharing your findings: writing up a project or making a presentation

The objectives of this chapter

This chapter aims to develop and support the skills you need for writing up a research project for an assignment or for publication, or as a presentation for colleagues and peers. It includes guidance on structuring your work; identifying the appropriate literature and writing a literature review, using online and offline sources of research literature, including online journals, professional publications and other published texts; and styles of writing, both scholarly and professional. It looks at ways research can be presented orally, to small audiences in meetings or to larger audiences at conferences. The chapter includes exemplar extracts from 'real' assignments, reports and presentations. As well as providing a template and example paragraphs for writing a review of your reading, it also sets out a straightforward guide to referencing.

The chapter will revisit some key research terminology, which by now you should be familiar with, such as: *dissemination; literature review; Harvard referencing.*

Introduction

Exciting as it is to carry out research and find answers to our questions, we mustn't lose sight of the purpose of educational inquiry, which is to inform and improve professional practice; both our own and others'. In order for our work to have an impact on teaching and learning beyond our own classrooms, we have to disseminate or share our research findings with colleagues, with the wider FE and training community, and possibly even with shareholders such as employers and policy makers. We can do this by writing up our research and publishing it in an academic journal or a professional journal or magazine; or by giving a local radio interview; or by presenting our work to an audience of colleagues or other professionals at conferences or in-house CPD days. The important thing is to share what we have discovered so that others may reflect on it and make use of it if they wish. *What* you disseminate – an account of your research and your findings – is one thing; *how* you present it is another. For example, the style of writing you use for an academic paper will be more formal than that required of an article for a professional magazine aimed at practitioners; and the detail you would include about your methodology would probably be greater in a slide presentation at an academic conference than at a CPD event for colleagues in your own department, where you might want to go into more detail about how your findings can be applied to practice. We're going to look in this chapter at writing up a section of a formal research paper or assignment; and at compiling a set of slides for presentation at a whole-college CPD event. Both of these involve disseminating your research to a fairly wide audience, some of whom will not necessarily share your subject expertise.

Structuring your research report

Whether you share your research through the publication of a paper or through a presentation to an audience of colleagues, you will need to structure your report in a way that enables others to understand exactly what you did and why; what you discovered and how you will use this in your professional practice. There is a widely accepted format for doing this which we can use for guidance. It divides the report into a logical sequence of sections, as follows:

Section of report or assignment	What it should contain
Introduction	In this opening section you need to explain to the reader or audience the context and the purpose of your research. This means that you must state your research question clearly and explain why you consider it important or useful to find an answer. To do this you will need to explain something about the context of your own professional practice, both in terms of teaching and learning and also, if appropriate, of current relevant developments in the FE sector as a whole.
A review of relevant literature	This is an important part of your report. Its purpose is to demonstrate that you have read around the topic that you're researching and that you are aware of what other researchers have already discovered about it. You can then make a link to your own research question. For example, you might explain that you want to discover whether your own findings agree with those in the literature; or, if there is more than one theory or explanation out there, you may point out that you're carrying out your own research to find out which of these it agrees with. It is important that the literature you review and discuss should be current or recent. This means that you will need to access research papers published in relevant academic journals.
Method and methodology	This is the section in which you explain *how* you collected your data (Method), and *why* you chose to do it that way (Methodology). Your methodology is the justification or rationale that you present for your chosen method. To write it convincingly you will need to make references to research theory, which you will have found, for example, in some of the recommended reading from this book, such as Cohen et al. (2011) or Wellington (2000).

This section should also include your explanation of how you have approached the analysis of your data; and again this should be supported by references to research literature. |
| Findings | Here is where you set out what you have found. When dealing with qualitative data, however, it is often more |

useful to combine this section with the next so that you can present, for example, your analysis of the responses to an open ended questionnaire and discuss their significance at the same time.

Discussion of findings

Whether or not you combine this section with the previous one, you should be sure to show how your own findings relate to a) your research question and b) to the research literature you have reviewed. Whose research do your findings appear to confirm? Do your findings appear to contradict any you have previously reviewed?

Conclusions

There are several points to be covered in your conclusion. For example:

- Summary of the findings.
- How they will apply to your own professional practice.
- Their implications for your college or organisation's policy and practices.
- Anything about your research you would wish to have done differently.
- How you would like to follow up this research if you had the opportunity.

List of references

You should list in alphabetical order of author surname all the references you have used in the text of your report. The usual way to do this for educational research is by using the Harvard referencing system, which we shall discuss later in this chapter. You can look up these conventions online; and you will, of course, see what these look like in practice in the research papers you read as part of your literature review.

Appendices

If you are using appendices, remember that they come after the list of references. Appendices can be useful if you want to include non-essential but helpful contextual material. If you do use appendices you should make sure you number them carefully and refer to them where appropriate in your report. There's no point just sticking an appendix on the end if it's never mentioned.

Literature review

We're going to look in more detail now at compiling a literature review, by examining an example written as part of an assignment paper. One of the most important things to remember is that the literature review is a means of showing where your own research fits into the existing published research on the same topic. It allows you to explain and offer a critical analysis of relevant and related research, and to use this as a point of comparison for your own methodology and your own findings. When planning your literature review there are three important factors to consider:

1. *Sources of literature.* Papers in academic journals are the best guide to what is current in your field of research. But online sources can be very useful, too. Be sure to make a note of full references as you go along. This will save you a lot of time and frustration when it comes to compiling your reference list. If there appears to very little literature on your chosen topic, spread your search more widely. If there's nothing relating to FE, for example, perhaps there's something relevant relating to schools; or to vocational education in another country. You can then explain in your review why you have had to extend your search in this way. This has the advantage of demonstrating that your own research is timely and useful because it fills what would otherwise be a gap.

2. *Themes.* Writing about what you have read can seem a difficult task in terms of organisation. A useful way to impose some logical structure on what you have to say is to identify key themes in the literature and to use these as sub-headings under which you can organise your review. You can then refer back to these themes when you are analysing and presenting your findings, to show whether or to what extent your own research reflects what others have had to say about these key areas.

3. *Critical analysis.* It is not enough to simply describe what you have read. A literature review which goes along the lines of, *'So and so said this; and another so and so said this'* and so on, is not a review at all; it is more like a shopping list. To avoid this, you need to do three things:

   - **Compare one source with another. To what extent do they agree? To what extent do they differ?**
   - **Show how this source relates to your research question. What light does it shine on it? Has the writer arrived at an answer by the same research method you have used, or in a different way?**
   - **Take a critical and analytical approach. For example, if the writer is presenting the outcome of some research, how wide was their sample? Do they tell you? If not, what are the implications? How reliable was their method of gathering data? If the writer is presenting an argument, do they offer supporting evidence? Do they argue logically? To what extent does their argument agree with what you know from your own professional experience?**

TASK TASK TASK TASK **TASK** TASK TASK TASK **TASK** TASK

Below you will find a literature review written by Desmond as part of his research assignment. As you read it through, notice how he has:

1) identified key themes in the relevant literature;

2) related these to his research question;

3) presented clear references to the literature he has cited in the form of author and date;

4) used the form 'et al.' to abbreviate the list of authors for multi-authored texts. (The names of all the authors involved will, of course, be listed in his references at the end of his report, as you will see.)

The review is not perfect, however. So, imagine now that it is your own work and you are proofreading before submitting it. See whether you can spot four errors that have been made, and note down what you would do to correct each of them. To help you, here are some clues:

i.   The absence of a reference to support a general point or claim.

ii. A cut and paste error.

iii. Unnecessarily including full title and publisher in a reference within the text.

iv. Lapsing into polemic.

Desmond. Section 2: Literature Review

In searching for literature relevant to my research question: 'How can teachers in FE best support learners with dyslexia?' I could find very little research on the topic which related specifically to the FE sector. Therefore I widened my search and have also drawn on literature relating to learners with dyslexia in schools and to dyslexia in general. In order to ensure that the literature was current, I also did a search of available sources online. Over all, four main themes emerge: Public understanding and misunderstanding of dyslexia; implications for learning and how dyslexia can affect learners' confidence; implications for teachers' professional practice; and implications for assessing written work. I have discussed each of these separately, before summarising the literature as a whole in relation to the research question.

Public understanding and misunderstanding of what dyslexia means

It has been argued that the majority of problems to do with dyslexia being supported within education stem from the misunderstanding of dyslexia by the majority of people, who are unaffected by it (Goodwin and Thomson, 2004; Chambers, 2009 [online]). Tutors need the knowledge of this learning difficulty, the ways in which we can best offer support and put provisions in place within our classrooms. Goodwin and Thomson (2004) argue that around 50 per cent of students in Further and Higher Education who have dyslexia are unaware of this or do not declare it, making it difficult to provide appropriate institutional support. Since this source is almost a decade old, however, it cannot be assumed that this same percentage still applies. Clearly, however, it is important that teachers should be aware that there may be learners in their classes who are disadvantaged by dyslexia without being able to put a name to their difficulty.

Implications for learning

The literature offers a number of ideas for creating an inclusive learning environment for dyslexic students. Holloway (2000), for example, focuses on classroom seating arrangements and layout, arguing that seating in rows should be avoided, and emphasising the need for teacher eye contact with every learner. This is reiterated by Pavey et al. (2010), whose checklist for setting up an inclusive classroom also includes the desirability of peer support and quiet areas. Reid (2005), on the other hand, emphasises the need for differentiation by learning experience, ensuring that learners are supported in taking different routes, according to their needs, to achieve the same outcomes. Similarly, Holloway (2000) stresses the need for teachers to adopt a flexible, learner-centred approach, in which they demonstrate a willingness to adapt their teaching styles to learner needs, since learners with dyslexia are particularly dependent on this type of flexibility of learning opportunity. In fact it is unbelievable and an utter disgrace that any teacher would not have the sense and sensitivity to do that.

How dyslexia can affect learners' confidence

Reid (2005, p.94) points out that: 'one of the most crucial elements in effective learning is self esteem', and this is a particular difficulty for learners with dyslexia, who may have a history of apparent 'failure' and embarrassment in formal learning situations. It is important therefore, as Pavey et al. (2010) point out in *Dyslexia-Friendly Further and Higher Education*. London: Sage, that teachers focus on building their confidence as well as their subject knowledge and understanding. This same point is implied by the British Dyslexia Association (2010 [online]) which points out that dyslexia can lead to a sense of social isolation in the classroom, which in turn can lead to stress and anxiety. This may be particularly the case in FE, since, as Holloway (2000) points out,

> *'It is not unusual for dyslexia to be discovered in the 16 plus age range. Those who do not have their dyslexia recognised until they are older may feel anger' (p.7).*

There are clear implications here for FE teachers, who may have to support and advise learners in such a situation.

Implications for teachers' professional practice

There is an emphasis in the literature on how an appropriate use of resources, both simple and complex, can improve the learning experience for learners with dyslexia. Mabel (2012) for example, suggests the use of simple post-its and coloured pens as an aid to learners' organisation, as well as software such as spellchecks and text readers and transcribers to support written work. Similarly, McNary et al. (2005) stress the need for teachers to ensure that learners are familiar with the range of technological support available. Pavey et al. (2010) suggest a number of practices teachers should observe when providing textual resources for learners with dyslexia. There are guidelines for the provision of textual support to learners with dyslexia (British Dyslexia Association, 2010), including the recommendation that they should be provided with summaries of lectures which they can read beforehand. Pavey et al. (2010) suggest a number of practices teachers should observe when providing textual resources for learners with dyslexia. These include using a rounded font in which letters can be easily distinguished; grouping text in paragraphs of no more than five lines; and using subheadings frequently as 'signposts'. Font is an issue also raised by Goodwin and Thomson (2004), who argue that these should be kept simple. Vickerman (2009) goes further, arguing for the use of illustrations as a useful way of supporting the written word.

All these place responsibility with the teacher. However, as Morgan and Klein (2000) point out, provision for dyslexic learners in FE and HE is usually offered in the form of specialised learning support. This suggests the need for a debate about whether teachers in FE should be reviewing their teaching in order to support such learners, or simply referring them to specialised support within the college.

Implications for assessing written work

This is a particular area of difficulty, as learners with dyslexia often find it difficult to proofread their own work productively. Moreover, they may be further disadvantaged by difficulties over note-taking and key word recognition. There is a question here about the extent to which accurate literacy skills are or should be a pre-requisite for demonstrating learning and understanding (Reid, 2005). Holloway (2000) argues that the content of learners' written work should be evaluated in its own right, regardless of errors in spelling and grammar. My view is that such errors are likely to hinder clear communication and therefore make content evaluation problematical. There is general agreement in the literature that learners with dyslexia need more time in which to complete their work. Goodwin and Thomson (2004) suggest that this may be largely due to the inability to organise and prioritise time and material, and that complex tasks such as assignments can appear overwhelmingly difficult. The implication here is that the teacher should find ways to break complex tasks down into smaller components.

Summary

On the whole, the literature not only discusses some of the key issues facing the teacher, but also proposes a range of strategies that the teacher might find of practical help in supporting learners with dyslexia. The two main unresolved debates appear to be: whether support should be a part of teachers' required role or be provided exclusively by specialists; and whether assessment should or could be based on solely on the content of written work.

Discussion

So, having seen how Desmond presents his literature review, let's check the effectiveness of your proofreading by discovering whether you spotted those minor errors:

i) The absence of a reference to support a general point or claim.
You may have noticed this early in the section headed *'Implications for assessing written work',* where Desmond writes: *'This is a particular area of difficulty, as learners with dyslexia often find it difficult to proofread their own work productively. Moreover, they may be further disadvantaged by difficulties over note-taking and key word recognition'.* Broad claims or generalised statements such as these two must be supported by references to appropriate sources, otherwise they are not admissible as support for the writer's argument.

ii) A cut and paste error
These are very common and only careful proofreading will reveal them because they are not usually highlighted by spell-checks. They creep into the text when you are editing and moving sentences and paragraphs around. You will almost certainly have seen where Desmond has failed to notice this in the section headed: *'Implications for teachers' professional practice'* where the following sentence occurs twice: *'Pavey et al. (2010) suggest a number of practices teachers should observe when providing textual resources for learners with dyslexia.'*

iii) Including full title and publisher in a reference within the text.
Within the text of your report or assignment, references should take the form of author's surname and date of publication; and should include the page number if you are quoting directly from this work. This enables the reader to look up the full detailed reference, giving publisher and place of publication, in the list of references at the end of your work, which will be arranged in alphabetical order of author surname to make this process simple for the reader. Desmond has cited references correctly in every instance except one, which occurs in the section headed: *'How dyslexia can affect learners' confidence'* and reads: *'It is important therefore, as Pavey et al. (2010) point out in* Dyslexia-Friendly Further and Higher Education. *London: Sage...'* All he needed here was Pavey et al. (2010). The other details are unnecessary as the reader should be able to find them in the final List of References.

iv) Lapsing into polemic
Desmond clearly feels very strongly about his subject, and at one point his otherwise clear and academic writing disappears and he gets up on his soapbox and starts using emotionally charged language. In fact it is the language which gives the game away that this is, for a moment, not just an academic argument for him. You'll almost certainly have spotted this one lapse at the end of the section headed *'Implications for learning'* where Desmond writes: *'In fact it is unbelievable and an utter disgrace that any teacher would not have the sense and sensitivity to do that'.* The language immediately identifies this as a 'rant': *'unbelievable'* and *'utter disgrace'.* And he begins it with the phrase *'In fact',* suggesting that there is no argument possible about this; that it is in some sense *true* – whereas of course we know that *facts* or *truth* are notoriously slippery concepts, even in the context of a cogent and evidence-based argument.

Feeling passionately about inclusion and social justice is an admirable thing. However, in a piece of academic writing, like this research report, such commitment is more effectively and appropriately expressed through compelling argument than through rhetoric. This doesn't mean that you cannot express your own view. Indeed, when researching matters relating to your own professional practice it is to be expected that you will have an informed view and that you will articulate it as part of your evaluation of the key arguments found in the literature. Desmond does just this towards the end when he writes: *'My view is that such errors are likely to hinder clear communication and therefore make content evaluation problematical.'* Here he states his view firmly, using measured language and identifying it clearly as his own viewpoint and not a blanket imperative.

CLOSE FOCUS CLOSE FOCUS **CLOSE FOCUS** CLOSE FOCUS **CLOSE FOCUS**

To what extent does Desmond's literature review:

- **take a critical and analytical approach?**
- **show how his sources relate to his research question?**
- **compare one source with another?**

Referencing

Desmond now has to set out in full the references to all those sources he has cited. He is using Harvard referencing conventions, which will make it straightforward for the reader to identify and find the original sources if they so wish. You'll find his list below. As you read through it, take careful note of the following:

- *The use of alphabetical order by author surname*, which enables the reader to find the full reference easily. (Imagine how frustrating it would be to find them listed in random order so that you would have to waste time searching through the lot to find what you were looking for.)
- *The punctuation*. There are very precise rules governing this. See whether you can work out what they are.
- *The emphasising of titles*. In Desmond's list this is done by the use of italics. You could also use bold or underlining. But whichever means of emphasis you choose, you should use it consistently throughout the list. 'Title' here means the title of an authored or edited book or a journal. Therefore when you are listing the author of a research paper published in a journal, it is not the title of the paper but of the journal that you must emphasise. Similarly, if you are listing the author of a chapter in an edited book, it is the book's title, not the chapter's, that must be emphasised. Look out for examples of these conventions in Desmond's list.
- *The place of publication for books*. This is given before the name of the publisher, and followed by a colon. You can usually find the publisher's address on the same page as the ISBN numbers at the beginning of the book.
- *The volume and number of the academic journal*. Such journals are published several times a year, so volume and number are important identifiers.
- *Date accessed for online sources*. Websites can change and disappear in a way that hard copy printed matter cannot. Therefore it is now a required convention of referencing that you state the date you last accessed an online source.

Desmond Literature review
References

Chambers, P. (2009) *Teachers and Dyslexia*. [Online] Available at http://www.gozunder/chambersr/poti/dyslexia.html (Accessed 05.05.2013)

Goodwin, D. and Thomson, V. (2004) *Making Dyslexia Work For You – A self-help guide*. London: David Fulton Publishers.

Holloway, J. (2000) *Dyslexia in Focus at Sixteen Plus – An inclusive teaching approach*. Tamworth: NASEN.

Mabel, T. (2012) *Including All Stakeholders.* London: Vlad Publishing.

McNary, S.J., Glasgow, N.A. and Hicks, C.D. (2005) *What Successful Teachers do in Inclusive Classrooms*. London: Sage.

Pavey, P., Meehan, M. and Waugh, A. (2010) *Dyslexia-Friendly Further and Higher Education*. London: Sage.

Reid, G. (2005) *Dyslexia and Inclusion – Classroom approaches for assessment, teaching and learning*. London: David Fulton Publishers.

The British Dyslexia Association (2010) *How FE and HE Tutors Can Help* [online]. Available at <http://www.bdadyslexia.org.uk/about-dyslexia/schools-colleges-and-universities/how-fe-he-tutors-can-help.html> [Accessed 05/05/2013]

Vickerman, E. (2009) Don't Write Dyslexics off. *The Teacher*. December 2009. p.50.

Now let's take two of the references he's listed and break them down into their constituent parts so that we can see how the rules of presentation apply to a) books and b) journal articles. First let's look at a single authored book:

Mabel, T. (2012) *Including All Stakeholders.* London: Vlad Publishing.

Author's name, surname first, followed by a comma and then the initial followed by a full stop.	Mabel, T.
Date of publication in brackets.	(2012)
Title of book, emphasised (in this case by using italics) and followed by a full stop.	*Including All Stakeholders.*
Place of publication, followed by a colon.	London:
Name of publisher, followed by a full stop.	Vlad Publishing.

However, when it comes to setting out the reference to a journal article the correct format is slightly different after the author's name and date. For example:

Vickerman, E. (2009) Don't Write Dyslexics off. *The Teacher*. December 2009. p.50.

Author's name, surname first, followed by a comma and then the initial followed by a full stop.	Vickerman, E.
Date of publication in brackets.	(2009)
Title of the article or paper in normal font, followed by a full stop.	Don't Write Dyslexics off.
Title of the publication or journal, emphasised (in this case by use of italics), followed by a full stop	*The Teacher.*
The issue and/or number of the publication, followed by a full stop.	December 2009.
The page or pages on which the article or paper can be found (in this case it's on one page only) followed by a full stop.	p.50.

Now look carefully at how a) a website reference; and b) a multi-authored book have been presented in Desmond's list. Using a grid like the one above, identify the punctuation and presentational conventions he has applied.

Preparing a presentation of your research

Let's assume that Desmond has now been asked to present his research at a CPD day for all college staff. This is a daunting prospect as there will be over 200 people in the audience. He decides to use a PowerPoint presentation to convey the main points. As he prepares the presentation he keeps two useful pointers in mind. The first is that he wants to have the same logical structure to his presentation as he used for his research assignment paper. The second is that, as an experienced teacher, he knows he must not crowd each slide.

Look at Desmond's first draft of his presentation opposite. Some of the slides (4, 7 and 12) are still blank. What would you advise him to put in there? Think carefully not only about the content, but also about how those slides should be worded. You may find it useful to make some notes so that you can compare your ideas with the suggestions in the discussion below.

Desmond's Presentation (see slides opposite)

Discussion

You'll have noticed that Desmond has left out the literature review. Sequentially, this would appear in slide 4. Perhaps he thought that it was too 'academic' for a presentation to colleagues; but it is important for him to show that this is an area of research which is relevant and current, and that there are findings and debates which have a bearing on his own question. Obviously, he wouldn't set out the literature in detail; but he could summarise the key themes. Slide 4 would then look something like this:

> Relevant Literature and
> Published Research
>
> Four themes:
> • Understandings and
>   misunderstandings
> • Learning and confidence
> • Implications for teaching
> • Implications for assessment

He has also omitted to say anything about his methodology. He's described the method he used but has given no reasons for why he made this choice, nor what its disadvantages might be. Slide 7 would be the appropriate place for this. It's important that he explains this, because it will allow him to demonstrate a) that he has made an informed choice; and b) that he is aware of potential criticisms, for example on the grounds of unreliability, and is able to answer them.

My research question "How can teachers in FE best support learners with dyslexia?"	**7.**
Context: why this question is important for me • My role: Business Studies Teacher • My learners: 14-19 year olds • My college: Large urban GFE college	**Findings 1: Teachers** • All 10 teachers claimed that they gave support. • 8 of them referred to specifics such as advanced notes, extra time, etc. • 1 of them said she provided learners with dyslexia with one-to-one tutorial support for written assignments in her own time. • 1 of them said he gave support in the form of "encouragement".
Context: Why this question is important to the college • Growing numbers of learners identified as having dyslexia • No formal support groups • Limited resources • No specialised staff training or awareness raising	**Findings 2: Learners** • 7 learners said they received no support specific to their dyslexia from teachers. • 3 learners said they were given extra time to complete assignments and advanced copies of all slide presentations. • 2 learners said that they were given one-to-one help by their teacher in her own time.
4	**Findings 3: Managers** • Both managers said that they expected staff to provide appropriate support in the form of extra time, advance copies of slides and handouts, and differentiated tasks broken down into stages. • 1 manager said she believed all her staff did this. • The other manager suggested that there should be appropriate CPD provided before staff could be expected to give appropriate support.
Method: How I collected my data • Interviews 10 teachers 10 learners with diagnosed dyslexia 2 managers (HoD Business Studies: HoD Media Studies)	**Summary of Findings** • All 10 teachers and 1 manager assume (or at least claim) that there is teacher support for all learners with dyslexia **BUT** • 7 out of 10 learners claim they do not receive support • 1 manager argues for CPD to raise staff awareness of how they can provide effective support.
Interview questions • I asked teachers an open question: "What do you do to support learners with dyslexia?" • I asked learners an open question: "What support to you receive from teachers for your dyslexia?" • I asked managers an open question: "What support do you expect teachers to give to learners with dyslexia?"	**12.**

So he might design slide 7 to look like this:

Interviews: who and why?

- Interviews allow open questions and possibility for clarification.
- Allows learners to talk, not write.
- Included all 10 learners with dyslexia in Dept.
- 10 staff were volunteers (therefore not necessarily representative).
- Additional HoD was to provide a point of comparison.

Slide 12 is also blank. Desmond could do one of several things here:

- **He could discuss the relevance of his findings to his own professional practice and explain how he will he use this research to inform his teaching.**
- **He could summarise the implications for whole college policy and practice.**
- **He could explain how he would follow this up with further research.**
- **Or he could do all three of these!**

CLOSE FOCUS CLOSE FOCUS **CLOSE FOCUS** CLOSE FOCUS **CLOSE FOCUS**

Choose one of the options above and design Desmond's final slide.

A SUMMARY OF **KEY POINTS**

In this chapter we have discussed:
> **why, as professionals, we need to share our research;**
> **how to structure a research report, assignment or presentation;**
> **how to write a literature review;**
> **how to set out your list of references;**
> **how to prepare an effective presentation of your research.**

We have also identified some useful terms to use when writing about documentary research. These include: *dissemination; literature review; Harvard referencing.*

Branching options

You may like to choose one of the following activities which are designed to help you apply what you've learnt from this chapter to your own practice. The first encourages you, as a professional, to develop your skills of reflection; the second asks you to take an evaluative approach consistent with an initial teaching qualification in the sector; and the third is designed to support skills of critical analysis appropriate to post-qualification CPD or Masters level study.

Reflection

Keeping in mind your current research project, look through a range of academic and professional journals to find one which seems to publish research on the same sort of topics and scale. You will find it useful to search both online and through any hard copy journals in your own institution's library to get an idea of the contents and themes. Remember that you can get a 'feel' for the content of the paper by reading the abstract, which can often be accessed online even when full content is not available.

Evaluation

Imagine you've been asked to present your current research project to the rest of your department on the next CPD day. Design a set of slides which summarise your research and explain its relevance to your own professional practice and to policy and practice within the college as a whole. You may find it useful to keep in mind the elements of Desmond's presentation that we have discussed in this chapter.

Critical analysis

Drawing on the reading you have done to date, draft a review of the literature relevant to your current research project. Remember to identify key themes and accurately cite your sources. Remember, too, to show clearly how the sources you refer to relate to your research question.

REFERENCES AND FURTHER READING

Another text you might find useful is:

Chapters 4 and 12 of Atkins, L. and Wallace, S. (2012) *Qualitative Research in Education*. London: BERA/Sage.

These chapters look in detail at writing a literature review and at various ways in which practitioner researchers have disseminated their research.

You will also find it useful to read other people's research disseminated in recent editions of journals such as *Research in Post-Compulsory Education* and the *Journal of Vocational Education.*

11

Putting it all together and writing your research assignment

The objectives of this chapter

This chapter is designed to bring together everything covered in the previous chapters and to show what this looks like in the form of a complete research report of the kind you might be required to write as an assignment. It also provides you with an opportunity to test your knowledge and understanding of the key points contained in previous chapters. (You should note that the 'references' used in the research report are fictional ones, created to provide an example of the range of sources you might use and the referencing conventions that apply.)

Introduction

As we saw in the previous chapter, reporting the purpose, process and outcome of your research is an essential part of research activity. For many of you, the first occasion on which you do this will be when you write up an assignment as part of your CPD or your initial professional qualification. The report which forms the focus for the chapter is a typical example of such an assignment, written by a teacher or trainee teacher and based on a small-scale inquiry conducted within the context of their own professional practice. It is not offered as a 'perfect' example, although the template it follows is a useful one to remember. It is presented rather as a means for you to exercise your analytical and critical faculties; to apply what you've learnt so far; to try out your proofreading skills; and to reflect on how you might have expressed, structured or explained some of this differently or better. After your initial reading to get a 'feel' for the report, you'll be asked to re-read while considering some key questions about the content and argument. Following a discussion of these, you'll have an opportunity to look at the 'marked' version of this assignment complete with the tutor's comments and suggestions.

The assignment is written by Kev, whom we met in Chapter 1. You'll perhaps remember that his research focused on learners' note-taking skills, or lack of them. Since then, in response to formative feedback from his tutor he has thought carefully about questions of validity and reliability and how he could re-phrase his question and improve his research design. This reflection has informed his research report, as you'll see below.

TASK TASK TASK TASK TASK **TASK** TASK TASK TASK **TASK** TASK

Read Kev's assignment through to familiarise yourself with his purpose, his approach and his findings. When you have finished you will find a series of questions to guide you through a careful re-reading.

Kev

Research Assignment

Title: How can 16–19-year-old learners' note-taking skills be improved?

Introduction

This focus of this assignment arises from my belief that learners need note-taking skills if they are to get the most out of their learning experience. For example, these skills allow them to summarise their own ideas or key points from their reading as well as the main points emerging from class discussion or a teacher's presentation or lecture. There is evidence to show that learners retain information more securely and for longer if they have made their own notes than if they are given notes or summaries by their teacher (Evans, 2011). During my initial period of teaching experience in FE, I quickly became aware that no one in my two groups of 16–18-year-old level 2 learners was making notes during our discussions or my presentations. At first I wondered whether this was because I was covering topics they were already familiar with, but when it became apparent that this was not the case, I suggested that make notes as I would be testing their recall by doing a quiz with them towards the end of the session. However, only a handful of learners in each group made any effort to do this. When I took in their 'notes' at the end of the session it was clear that even those who had made the attempt lacked the skill to do so effectively.

I would argue that this lack has a number of implications for the FE teacher tasked with supporting the learning of such learners. Firstly, it limits the range of methods that can be productively employed. For example, whole group discussion, a useful and potentially learner-centred strategy, may throw up ideas and information which are important and relevant, but which cannot reliably be predicted or even foreseen by the teacher, making it impossible to produce 'summary' notes in advance. If learners lack the skill to make a note of such ideas at the time, there is a risk they may be lost. Therefore, whole group discussion becomes a less productive, less creative learning experience than it could potentially be. The same is true of small group discussion, role play, simulation, case studies and all other methods where the teacher cannot reliably predict what will emerge and therefore cannot produce complete notes for the learners beforehand. This leads to the temptation to rely heavily on teacher presentations, lectures and structured question and answer, where topics can be reliably summarised beforehand and given as pre-prepared handouts at the end of the session. As a student teacher in FE I looked forward to the challenge of engaging learners with a range of methods which would make learning interesting and enjoyable. It quickly became apparent to me that in order to do so, I would have to find a way to address the question of note-taking.

Literature Review

I found that the literature on learners' note-taking skills falls into two main categories. Firstly there is a body of research which focuses on note-taking as an aspect of over all literacy; secondly there is literature which categorises note-taking as part of thinking skills. There appears to be no body of work which deals specifically with note-taking skills in relation to 16–18-year-old learners in FE, nor indeed to note-taking skills among FE learners of any age. All the literature I have reviewed below relates to teaching and learning in the UK. I did not extend my search to other English-speaking countries as the word limit for this assignment restricts the length of this literature section.

Note-taking as an aspect of literacy.

Bates and Preston (2012) suggest that note-taking is a form of 'precis' (p.130) or summary, and can only be achieved as a result of the 'comprehension and synthesis of given information' (p.136). This is consistent with what some of the literature on note-taking as a thinking skill suggests in the next section. It implies that note-taking is in some sense a higher order skill in that it requires the note-taker to 'process the words of another' (p.144), extract the core facts or ideas, and then express these in their own words. The relation to literacy skills is further argued by Mwaya and Chen (2011) who make the point that it is impossible for learners to re-express something in their own words if they lack the range of vocabulary or formal expression to do so. This suggests that the development of note-taking skills is itself dependent on a firm foundation of verbal skills, both written and spoken, which should be built up during the years of schooling, and therefore by implication calls into question whether such skills can be effectively acquired as a result of one teacher's short-term intervention at the post-school stage. Prior and Kurtz (2012), on the other hand, argue that note-taking is a practical skill which can be taught in an instrumental way by coaching the learner to identify key words in the original material. They do not agree that note-taking needs to involve any significant level of synthesis, and argue that it is simply an exercise in 'selective mimicry' like an echo. I categorise this as part of the 'literacy' argument, however, because of the component of word recognition involved.

Note-taking as an aspect of thinking skills

In some ways the two themes in the literature meet in the term 'comprehension'. Davy (2013) argues that note-taking is primarily an exercise in comprehension and that this is why learners who are able to take accurate notes have better retention and recall than those who are not. She also suggests that the ability to make informed choices (for example, about what or what not to include in one's notes) is an important thinking skill, rather than a matter of literacy. Javier (2012), too, stresses the thinking processes behind the practical act of note-taking, and summarises these as:

> 'hearing, reflecting, understanding, and selecting. All these stages precede the for-mulation of the note that will be made on the screen or on the page'. (p. 44)

Brantone and Pugh (2013) go further, arguing that disorganised thinking is a barrier to effective note-taking, and that without first nurturing thinking skills in his or her learners the teacher will find it impossible to help them develop effective note-taking skills. However, it is not clear from their paper what evidence they have to support this argument, nor how their small-scale inquiry with 20 learners led them to make this assertion.

Summary

Apart from Prior and Kurtz (2012), therefore, both strands of the literature suggest that note-taking is not a skill which can be easily taught or acquired without addressing other factors such as general levels of literacy or the ability to think clearly and make informed choices. The implications for my own plan to improve learners' note-taking skills were therefore quite serious.

Method

I gathered my data in two stages. Initially, I broke my research question down into two lines of enquiry:

- How many of the students had been taught to take notes?
- What alternative strategies do learners use to help them remember what has been taught?

My plan was to apply these two questions to both groups of level 2 learners. I saw this as a mixed methods approach (Cohen et all, 2011). The first question would be answered by quantitative data; the second by qualitative or descriptive data. I elicited the first set of data by asking for a show of hands, and the qualitative data by use of a very simple questionnaire which asked two questions:

1. 'What do you do to help yourself to remember what we have talked about and what you have learnt in this lesson?'
2. 'How well does it work for you and why?'

I later came to treat this as a pilot stage in my research, since I realised, on reflection, that my questions were flawed and based on assumptions. For example, asking how many had been taught to make notes did not give me useful data on how many were actually able to do it. And the questionnaire questions assumed that learners had some strategy in place which, as their responses showed, the majority clearly did not. Because of the questions I had chosen to ask, the data that I collected lacked validity (Wellington, 2000). That is, it was not the appropriate data I needed in order to answer my overall research question. This was a useful learning experience for me.

I began again, therefore, and re-designed my research plan and rephrased my research question, which I refer to as 'Stage 2'. I asked both groups of learners to make notes during my lesson with them on January 31st. There were 17 learners in one group and 21 in the other. I was covering the same topic with both groups. At the end of the session I collected in the 'notes' they had made. I had told them they need not put their names on these as I was not assessing them, only evaluating them. These sheets of notes gave me a clear idea of the level of their note-taking skills which varied from poor to non-existent. The following session with both groups I gave them a gapped handout with key words missing and asked them to use this for note-taking purposes. Towards the end of the lesson we discussed whether they had found these useful, and again I collected them in at the end for evaluation before returning them. We used these key word gapped handouts for two weeks until it was clear that everyone was able to use them with confidence. I then introduced the use of a handout where in addition to key words, other elements such as descriptors and concepts were missing. Again, we discussed how these were working and both groups used them for two weeks to build confidence. Finally I taught a session with each group and asked them again to make notes, this time without the help of gapped handouts. My intention was that by building confidence and by encouraging recognition of key words and concepts I would be providing the learners with a supportive scaffolding which would eventually enable them to identify and note important points without that help. In terms of method, I would describe this as sort of experiment. It has elements of an action research approach (McNiff et al., 1996) in that I was identifying a problem and trying out an intervention to address it. Because I had only a limited time in my placement I was only able to complete one cycle of this research model. That is, I made one intervention (over time) and evaluated the outcome.

Methodology

While the first or pilot stage of my research had methodological flaws in terms of validity, the second stage was designed to produce data which was both reliable and valid (Wellington, 2000). In terms of action research, I could be reasonably confident of a causal link between my intervention – the progressive use of gapped handouts – and the outcome as measured by learner performance (Cohen et al., 2011). The answers to the questions I asked in the first stage could not necessarily be treated as trustworthy or reliable, because the power relationship between myself and the learners meant that there was always the risk that they might be giving me answers which they thought I wanted or which would impress me (Atkins and Wallace, 2012). Also, such answers rely on the participants' memory and on their willingness to tell the truth (Opie, 2004). In the second stage, however, my evaluation of the outcome was based on the quality of the learners' notes. There was, of course, the risk of researcher subjectivity in my evaluation of these – the danger that I would 'see' improvement because I wanted to and was specifically looking for it (Atkins and Wallace, 2012). But the notes also speak for themselves as evidence of my findings.

In conducting this research I was mindful of the BERA (2011) ethical guidelines for educational researchers, and ensured that I obtained informed consent from all the learners involved to be participants with me in this research experiment.

Findings

As mentioned in the introduction to this paper, the learners' note-taking skills, when sampled in Stage 1 of this research, were found to be generally poor and in most cases non-existent. Following the four-week intervention in which first very simple, keyword gapped handouts, and then more challenging handouts with more complex and challenging 'gaps' were used, the learners' lesson notes, made with no support, were found on the whole to be adequate and in some cases good. Out of the total of 38 learners, three learners were absent on the final day of the experiment; six still appeared unable to take useful or intelligible notes; but the remaining 29 learners produced notes which represented an adequate and accurate summary of the topic covered, which in four cases demonstrated quite complex note-taking skills.

These findings suggest that note-taking skills can be developed in learners who have no prior skills or experience in this area. This appears to support Prior and Kurtz's (2012) argument that note-taking is a practical skill which can be taught by coaching the learner to identify key words and concepts. It also appears to contradict the argument put forward by researchers such as Brantone and Pugh (2013) that note-taking skills cannot be effectively taught unless learners' thinking skills are addressed first.

Conclusion

This research will be helpful to me in my professional practice because it has demonstrated for me a way to encourage and support learners in taking notes, and this in turn will allow me to employ a wider range of teaching and learning methods to make their learning experience more engaging and dynamic.

I hope to present my research at the next College CPD day, as I believe my findings will be useful to other teachers across other vocational areas. If I had an opportunity to continue this research I would try out the same strategies with learners in different vocational areas and at different levels of qualification. It would also be interesting to try the strategy with adult learners.

References

Questions for guided reading

- Does the title convey accurately the focus and scale of the research?
- How does Kev use his account of the false start he made to his research to good effect in this assignment?
- Does Kev's introduction make the context and purpose of his research clear?
- Look carefully at how he has structured his literature review. Does it appear logical and clear? Are there any suggestions you would make for improvement?
- To what extent do you think the literature review takes a critical and analytical approach to the literature? Can you identify any examples of critical analysis?
- Has Kev made any use of, or reference to, this literature later in his report?
- Can you identify any points in the report which seem insufficiently developed and where more information would be helpful to the reader?
- Look at how Kev has structured his conclusion. What has he included? Is there anything else he could have covered here?
- What other points, if any, do you think Kev's tutor will be likely to comment on?
- If this were your own assignment, what revisions would you make in order to improve it?
- If you have not done this already, proofread the assignment closely now and mark up any errors or typos that you notice. Remember, it's always easier to spot mistakes in someone else's work

because we are able to read it with an objective eye. If you can bring this same sense of objectivity to proofreading your own work, you will find you do it much more effectively.

Discussion

Now we are going to look at what Kev's tutor has said about Kev's work. She has used comment boxes, and so we can see very clearly exactly what section, phrase or word each comment is referring to. As you read this feedback, compare it with the notes you made about your own responses to the questions above. Has the tutor pointed out anything that you missed? If so, what might you learn from her comment? And did you find any areas of weakness or room for improvement which the tutor seems to have missed?

Marked assignment with tutor's comments

Kev

Research Assignment

Title: How can 16-19-year-old learners' note-taking skills be improved?

Comment [S1]: You need to make the scale of your research clear in your title. You are not looking at ALL 16-19 year olds, but 16-19 year olds on a level 2 vocational programme in an FE college.

Introduction

This focus of this assignment arises from my belief that learners need note-taking skills if they are to get the most out of their learning experience. For example, these skills allow them to summarise their own ideas or key points from their reading as well as the main points emerging from class discussion or a teacher's presentation or lecture. There is evidence to show that learners retain information more securely and for longer if they have made their own notes than if they are given notes or summaries by their teacher (Evans, 2011). During my initial period of teaching experience in FE, I quickly became aware that no one in my two groups of 16–18-year-old level 2 learners was making notes during our discussions or my presentations. At first I wondered whether this was because I was covering topics they were already familiar with, but when it became apparent that this was not the case, I suggested that make notes as I would be testing their recall by doing a quiz with them towards the end of the session. However, only a handful of learners in each group made any effort to do this. When I took in their 'notes' at the end of the session it was clear that even those who had made the attempt lacked the skill to do so effectively.

Comment [S2]: In your title you say "16-19". You should proof read carefully for errors such as this.

Comment [S3]: Word missing here. Again, an indication that you need to PROOF READ more carefully!

I would argue that this lack has a number of implications for the FE teacher tasked with supporting the learning of such learners. Firstly, it limits the range of methods that can be productively employed. For example, whole group discussion, a useful and potentially learner-centred strategy, may throw up ideas and information which are important and relevant, but which cannot reliably be predicted or even foreseen by the teacher, making it impossible for the teacher to produce 'summary' notes in advance. If learners lack the skill to make a note of such ideas at the time, there is a risk they may be lost. Therefore, whole group discussion becomes a less productive, less

Comment [S4]: A good point. But wouldn't a plenary allow key points to be identified?

creative learning experience than it could potentially be. The same is true of small group discussion, role play, simulation, case studies and all other methods where the teacher cannot reliably predict exactly what ideas or arguments will emerge and therefore cannot produce notes for the learners beforehand. This leads to the temptation to rely heavily on teacher presentations, lectures and structured question and answer, where topics can be reliably summarised beforehand and given as pre-prepared handouts at the end of the session. As a student teacher in FE I looked forward to the challenge of engaging learners with a range of methods which would make learning interesting and enjoyable. It quickly became apparent to me that in order to do so, I would have to find a way to address the question of note-taking.

> **Comment [S5]:** Unclear. Do you mean it tempts the TEACHER to rely too heavily on lectures, etc?

> **Comment [S6]:** Good point. You've explained how and why your research is relevant to your professional practice.

Literature Review

I found that the literature on learners' note-taking skills falls into two main categories. Firstly there is a body of research which focuses on note-taking as an aspect of over all literacy; secondly there is literature which categorises note-taking as part of thinking skills. There appears to be no body of work which deals specifically with note-taking skills in relation to 16–18-year-old learners in FE, nor indeed to note-taking skills among FE learners of any age. All the literature I have reviewed below relates to teaching and learning in the UK. I did not extend my search to other English-speaking countries as the word limit for this assignment restricts the length of this literature section.

> **Comment [S7]:** Is this a valid reason? Are there other, more valid reasons you might have given for excluding this wider literature from your search?

Note-taking as an aspect of literacy.

Bates and Preston (2012) suggest that note-taking is a form of 'precis' (p.130) or summary, and can only be achieved as a result of the 'comprehension and synthesis of given information' (p.136). This is consistent with what some of the literature on note-taking as a thinking skill suggests in the next section. It implies that note-taking is in some sense a higher order skill in that it requires the note-taker to 'process the words of another' (p.144), extract the core facts or ideas, and then express these in their own words. The relation to literacy skills is further argued by Mwaya and Chen (2011) who make the point that it is impossible for learners to re-express something in their own words if they lack the range of vocabulary or formal expression to do so. This suggests that the development of note-taking skills is itself dependent on a firm foundation of verbal skills, both written and spoken, which should be built up during the years of schooling, and therefore by implication calls into question whether such skills can be effectively acquired as a result of one teacher's short-term intervention at the post-school stage. Prior and Kurtz (2012), on the other hand, argue that note-taking is a practical skill which can be taught in an instrumental way by coaching the learner to identify key words in the original material. They do not agree that note-taking needs to involve any significant level of synthesis, and argue that it is simply an exercise in 'selective mimicry' like an echo. I categorise this as part of the 'literacy' argument, however, because of the component of word recognition involved.

> **Comment [S8]:** This would make a good linking point between the two sections. In terms of organising your material, it would have been better to discuss this source last in this section so it could be a logical lead into the section about thinking skills.

> **Comment [S9]:** This seems to be the approach you have taken in your "experiment" and yet you do not refer back to Prior and Kurtz when explaining your method. You would have gained extra marks for doing so.

Note-taking as an aspect of thinking skills

In some ways the two themes in the literature meet in the term 'comprehension'. Davy (2013) argues that note-taking is primarily an exercise in comprehension and that this is why learners who are able to take accurate notes have better retention and recall than those who are not. She also suggests that the ability to make informed choices (for example, about what or what not to include in one's notes) is an important thinking skill, rather than a matter of literacy. Javier (2012), too, stresses the thinking processes behind the practical act of note-taking, and summarises these as:

> *'hearing, reflecting, understanding, and selecting. All these stages precede the formulation of the note that will be made on the screen or on the page.'* (p. 44)

> **Comment [S10]:** Good. You've set this quote out clearly and distinguished it from your own words by insetting, and using italics. It is not wrong to also use quotation marks, but not strictly necessary in this case as you have used these other ways of showing it is a quote.

Brantone and Pugh (2013) go further, arguing that disorganised thinking is a barrier to effective note-taking, and that without first nurturing thinking skills in his or her learners the teacher will find it impossible to help them develop effective note-taking skills. However, it is not clear from their paper what evidence they have to support this argument, nor how their small-scale inquiry with 20 learners led them to make this assertion.

> **Comment [S11]:** Good! You are engaging critically with the lliterature here.

Summary

Apart from Prior and Kurtz (2012), therefore, both stands of the literature suggest that note-taking is not a skill which can be easily taught or acquired without addressing other factors such as general levels of literacy or the ability to think clearly and make informed choices. The implications for my own plan to improve learners' note-taking skills were therefore quite serious.

> **Comment [S12]:** This is a useful summary as far as it goes. But you should explain fully what these "implications" are. It's important, in a research report, to develop each point fully rather than assuming the reader will guess what you mean.

Method

I gathered my data in two stages. Initially, I broke my research question down into two lines of enquiry:

- How many of the students had been taught to take notes?
- What alternative strategies do learners use to help them remember what has been taught?

My plan was to apply these two questions to both groups of level 2 learners. I saw this as a mixed methods approach (Cohen et all, 2011). The first question would be answered by quantitative data; the second by qualitative or descriptive data. I elicited the first set of data by asking for a show of hands, and the qualitative data by use of a very simple questionnaire which asked two questions:

1. *'What do you do to help yourself to remember what we have talked about and what you have learnt in this lesson?'*

2. *'How well does it work for you and why?'*

I later came to treat this as a pilot stage in my research, since I realised, on reflection, that my questions were flawed and based on assumptions. For example, asking how many had been taught to make notes did not give me useful data on how many were actually able to do it. And the questionnaire questions assumed that learners had some strategy in place which, as their responses

> **Comment [S13]:** Good. In critically analysing your own approach and explaining why and how you revised it, you demonstrate that you understand and can now apply those concepts of reliability and validity.

showed, the majority clearly did not. Because of the questions I had chosen to ask, the data that I collected lacked validity (Wellington, 2000). That is, it was not the appropriate data I needed in order to answer my overall research question. This was a useful learning experience for me.

I began again, therefore, and re-designed my research plan and rephrased my research question, which I refer to as 'Stage 2'. I asked both groups of learners to make notes during my lesson with them on January 31st. There were 17 learners in one group and 21 in the other. I was covering the same topic with both groups. At the end of the session I collected in the 'notes' they had made. I had told them they need not put their names on these as I was not assessing them, only evaluating them. These sheets of notes gave me a clear idea of the level of their note-taking skills which varied from poor to non-existent. The following session with both groups I gave them a gapped handout with key words missing and asked them to use this for note-taking purposes. Towards the end of the lesson we discussed whether they had found them useful, and again I collected them in at the end for evaluation before returning them. We used these key word gapped handouts for two weeks until it was clear that everyone was able to use them with confidence. I then introduced the use of a handout where in addition to key words, other elements such as descriptors and concepts were missing. Again, we discussed how these were working and both groups used them for two weeks to build confidence. Finally I taught a session with each group and asked them again to make notes, this time without the help of gapped handouts. My intention was that by building confidence and by encouraging recognition of key words and concepts I would be providing the learners with a supportive scaffolding which would eventually enable them to identify and note important points without that help. In terms of method, I would describe this as sort of experiment. It has elements of an action research approach (McNiff et al., 1996) in that I was identifying a problem and trying out an intervention to address it. Because I had only a limited time in my placement I was only able to complete one cycle of this research model. That is, I made one intervention (over time) and evaluated the outcome.

Comment [S14]: Unclear. Do you mean the re-phrased question is "Stage 2"?

Comment [S15]: So presumably they did put their names to these?

Methodology

While the first or pilot stage of my research had methodological flaws in terms of validity, the second stage was designed to produce data which was both reliable and valid (Wellington, 2000). In terms of action research, I could be reasonably confident of a causal link between my intervention – the progressive use of gapped handouts – and the outcome as measured by learner performance (Cohen et al., 2011). The answers to the questions I asked in the first stage could not necessarily be treated as trustworthy or reliable, because the power relationship between myself and the learners meant that there was always the risk that they might be giving me answers which they thought I wanted or which would impress me (Atkins and Wallace, 2012). Also, such answers rely on the participant's memory and on their willingness to tell the truth (Opie, 2004). In the second stage, however, my evaluation of the outcome was based on the quality of the learners' notes. There was, of course, the risk of researcher subjectivity in my evaluation of these – the danger that I would 'see' improvement because I wanted to and was specifically looking for it (Atkins and Wallace, 2012). But the notes also speak for themselves as evidence of my findings.

> **Comment [S16]:** What about the discussions you say you had with learners when you were evaluating the handouts towards the end of the lessons? Couldn't you treat these evaluations as part of the data? What might be the advantages and disadvantages of doing so? How reliable would such data be?

In conducting this research I was mindful of the BERA (2011) ethical guidelines for educational researchers, and ensured that I obtained informed consent from all the learners involved to be participants with me in this research experiment. _ _ _ _ _ _ _ _ _ _ _ _ _ _

> **Comment [S17]:** How was this done?

Findings

As mentioned in the introduction to this paper, the learners' note-taking skills, when sampled in Stage 1 of this research, were found to be generally poor and in most cases non-existent. Following the four-week intervention in which first very simple, keyword gapped handouts, and then more challenging handouts with more complex and challenging 'gaps' were used, the learners' lesson notes, made with no support, were found on the whole to be adequate and in some cases good. Out of the total of 38 learners, three learners were absent on the final day of the experiment; six still appeared unable to take useful or intelligible notes; but the remaining 29 learners produced notes which represented an adequate and accurate summary of the topic covered which in four cases demonstrated quite complex note-taking skills.

> **Comment [S18]:** How, as a researcher, would you want to follow this up? Do you have any theories about why your strategy did not work for these learners?

These findings suggest that note-taking skills can be developed in learners who have no prior skills or experience in this area. This appears to support Prior and Kurtz's (2012), argument that note-taking is a practical skill which can be taught by coaching the learner to identify key words and concepts. It also appears to contradict the argument put forward by researchers such as Brantone and Pugh (2013) that note-taking skills cannot be effectively taught unless learners' thinking skills are addressed first. _ _ _ _ _ _ _ _ _ _ _ _ _ _

> **Comment [S19]:** Excellent! You have related your findings to the relevant literature discussed earlier. This is characteristic of a good research paper.

Conclusion

This research will be helpful to me in my professional practice because it has demonstrated for me a way to encourage and support learners in taking notes, and this in turn will allow me to employ a wider range of teaching and learning methods to make their learning experience more engaging and dynamic.

I hope to present my research at the next College CPD day, as I believe my findings will be useful to other teachers across other vocational areas. If I had an opportunity to continue this research I would try out the same strategies with learners in different vocational areas and at different levels of qualification. It would also be interesting to try the strategy with adult learners.

References

> **CLOSE FOCUS** CLOSE FOCUS **CLOSE FOCUS** CLOSE FOCUS **CLOSE FOCUS**
>
> Kev's list of references is not included here. You may find it useful practice to take all the writers he has referred to and arrange those names in alphabetical order.

Writing an abstract

You will no doubt have noticed, if you have been looking at published research papers, that they are preceded by an *abstract*. The abstract is a summary of the paper and it is useful to readers and other researchers because it allows them to see at a glance whether the contents of the paper are of relevance or interest to them. Abstracts are usually between 150 and 250 words. For the purposes of writing one, you could break that down into four complex sentences of roughly equal length which summarise:

1. What the topic is and why (summarising your Introduction).
2. The academic context (summarising the key themes in your Literature Review).
3. The method you used and sample size (summarising your Method section).
4. The key finding/s (summarising your Findings section).

It is perhaps surprising that Kev has not included an abstract, given that he seems to be interested in the whole process of summarising! But you now have an opportunity to write one for him.

> **TASK** TASK **TASK** TASK **TASK TASK** TASK **TASK** TASK **TASK TASK** TASK
>
> 1. First read carefully a selection of abstracts, using online sources or hard copy academic journals from your college or university library. Notice how they generally follow the format set out above.
> 2. Now write Kev's abstract for him, keeping in mind the ultimate purpose of the abstract which is to provide an accurate summary of the paper's context and argument.

Branching options

You may like to choose one of the following activities which are designed to help you apply what you've learnt from this chapter to your own practice. The first encourages you, as a professional, to develop your skills of reflection; the second asks you to take an evaluative approach consistent with an initial teaching qualification in the sector; and the third is designed to support skills of critical analysis appropriate to post-qualification CPD or Masters level study.

Reflection

Kev has made reference to a number of authors who write about research methods. These are: Wellington, 2000; Opie, 2004; Atkins and Wallace, 2012; Cohen et al., 2011; Whitehead and McNiff, 2006. These should be familiar to you now, as they have already been cited elsewhere in this book. Set out these references for him correctly, in full and in alphabetical order as they should appear in his reference list. You will find the full references (author/s, date, title, place of publication, publisher) set out at the end of various chapters. This is an exercise in accurate transcription as well as practice in the presentation of references.

Evaluation

Read Kev's paper through again carefully in order to evaluate the method and methodology sections. Has he explained sufficiently well his reasons for using the data collection method he chose? Has he acknowledged the possible disadvantages of this method? What, if anything, would you advise him to add or revise in these two sections?

Critical analysis

Read through Kev's paper again as though proofreading your own work, and identify any places where you think the argument could be strengthened, the approach could be more analytical, or the writing or content improved in any way. Make notes of the additions or revisions you would make.

REFERENCES AND FURTHER READING

The most useful reading you can do to reinforce and explore what you have learnt in this chapter is to be found in recent and current academic and professional journals, both hard copy and electronic, which publish research reports, papers and articles. An online search will show you where you can find papers relevant to your own area of focus or expertise. Two journals you may find particularly useful to look at are:

Research in Post-Compulsory Education
and
Research in Vocational Education and Training.

Index

Added to a page number 'f' denotes a figure and 't' denotes a table.